Medicine Maid

To the Delaware Nation who made Mary
one of their own.

MEDICINE MAID

The Life Story of a Canadian Pioneer

Illustrated by the Author

E. L. HOOPLE

Mika Publishing Company
Belleville, Ontario
1977

FC3071.1. H66H66   971.3'02'0924   C77-001399-6   F1058. H66H66
Printed and bound in Canada.

CONTENTS

FOREWORD

This is a true story which begins in Pennsylvania in 1779. Most of the people in it were real people and are called by their own names. However, there are exceptions. For instance, the first name of one of Mary's brothers is still a mystery. The historians called him only "the boy in the sugar bush". For the purpose of this book we have named him Jake.

In the course of over ten years of research no less than seven written versions of the Whitmore massacre were unearthed. These contained minor contradictions which had to be resolved and there were gaps in the records which had to be filled by a mixture of imagination and careful study of authoritative books, such as David Zeisberger's *History of Northern Indians*.

All the places mentioned in the story were visited. Reference libraries in Albany, Buffalo, Geneseo, Lansing, Detroit and Toronto yielded valuable material. It is amazing how much can be found and reconstructed after nearly two hundred years.

At Jerseytown, Pennsylvania, they will show the visitor the site of the Whitmore cabin and the spring where Mary went for water. In the museum at Geneseo, New York, is a rustic highchair that was made for Sarah Whitmore Jones' first baby. In the Fort George Museum at Niagara, Ontario, is preserved a beaded purse given to John Whitmore by his Indian mother. In the Three Counties Museum in Cornwall, Ontario, is the little porcelain bowl that Mary used to carry salve in her saddle-bags when she rode out to doctor the sick. The house that Mary and Henry built is still standing on the Second Concession of Osnabruck near the village of Long Sault, Ontario, and Henry's and Mary's tombstones are to be seen at Upper Canada Village.

My heartfelt thanks go to all those people, too numerous to mention, who helped collect the data for this book.

Streetsville, Ontario
    July, 1977

Elizabeth Hoople

Chapter I

THE WARNING

Bright autumn sunshine streamed through the open cabin door onto the bakeboard where Mary, her tongue tucked into one pink cheek and her long tawny-coloured pigtails tossed back out of the way, was firmly kneading a batch of dough.

Her three older sisters were setting out the finished loaves, putting last night's rising into the copper kettle over the coals to bake, and placing the new dough in the bread-box to rise. None of them could resist taking part in this special event - their first baking with wheat flour since coming to Pennsylvania. That year their father, Peter Whitmore, had grown wheat as well as corn in his clearing, and, although most of the small crop had to be saved for next year's seed, he had been able to spare a little for this family treat.

"I have not tasted white bread since we left New Jersey," said Sarah.

"And that must have been nearly five years ago," added Catherine.

As they worked, their three small brothers - Peter, George, and Johnny - attracted by the tantalizing smell of the baking, buzzed in and out of the cabin like wasps around a honey pot.

Suddenly a deep shadow fell across the bakeboard

and Mary looked up to see a familiar Indian silhouetted in the doorway. He was untying the carcass of a deer, and as she watched he lifted it from his shoulders and stooped to place it on the doorstep.

"Killbuck," exclaimed her mother, stepping forward to greet the big Delaware. "Welcome!" and she immediately reached for one of the golden loaves and handed it to him. He accepted gravely.

The deer, as they all knew, was a thank offering for hospitality received in the past, for Killbuck had often stayed overnight with them, sleeping wrapped in his blanket on the floor in front of the hearth. He and the other local Delawares were friends of the Whitmore family. From them Mary's father had bought his land, and he had remained on good terms with them ever since.

Today Killbuck seemed to be preoccupied. When he had eaten the loaf, he motioned for attention and began to speak in broken English. Holding up three fingers he said, "Lenni-Lenape one nation – three tribes." Then, stretching both arms before him, he repeated with emphasis, "Three tribes." Pointing with his right hand at them, at the carcass, and at himself, he said, "One Lenni-Lenape tribe – friends." Then, dramatically moving his left arm sideways and pointing towards the forest beyond the open door, he added solemnly, "Two Lenni-Lenape tribes NO friends."

Suddenly he was gone.

"Well!" exclaimed Sarah, "what on earth did he mean by that?"

Mrs. Whitmore sank abruptly onto a stool, looking white and strained. "I think he meant to warn us of danger from some of his Lenni-Lenape or Delaware people."

"Were they the ones who massacred the men at

Muncy?" asked Ann.

"I don't know. But I do know one thing, from now on you girls must stay within sight of the house. No more wandering off into the bush."

On a glorious autumn day not long after this, the various members of the family dispersed in separate groups to attend to the work of the farm. Peter Whitmore, with his two eldest sons, Phillip and Jake, set off for the east boundary of their land to build a fence. Sarah and Catherine elected to help their mother make soap, while the two younger girls decided it was high time to gather the family's winter supply of nuts.

Mary and Ann set forth gaily in search of nut-bearing trees – hickory, walnut and bur oak. Like the squirrels, they scampered light-heartedly through a carpet of crisp fallen leaves. Above them the scarlet of maple and the gold of birch leaves reflected the sunlight. They felt happy and care-free, enmeshed in a golden glow. Around them little blackcaps called sweetly to each other, "Chick adee dee dee," and there was a flash of vivid colour as two bluejays played tag in the tree tops. Following the course of the creek downstream to the west the girls came to a few hickory trees at the edge of a little ravine.

"We must stop here," said Ann. "If we go into the ravine we will no longer be in sight of the house."

They picked what hickory nuts they could find, but when they finished their skin bags were only half full. Disappointed, they gazed longingly across the ravine to its farther slope where stood a goodly clump of bur oaks laden with sweet acorns.

"I tell you what we can do, Ann. You stay here and I will go over there and keep an eye on you. That will be almost the same as being 'in sight of the house'. You will see the house and I will see you! Besides it is broad daylight; surely there can be no danger in the middle of the day."

Ann looked dubious but agreed to stay, and Mary skipped off into the ravine and up the opposite slope to the clump of bur oaks. There was a good crop of acorns, each one encircled by its green frill of fuzz, and Mary picked steadily for half an hour gathering all she could find on the lower branches. Then she climbed a tree to reach for more nuts higher up.

From this vantage point she could see for some distance. All at once, farther downstream, a flock of birds rose en masse into the air as though they had been frightened by something unusual in the forest below them. Mary froze on her perch. Was there danger down there? Someone approaching silently? Could there be enemy Indians coming towards her? At once she knew that she had done wrong in coming so far. She was not "in sight of the house." Her heart smote her as she realized that she might have endangered not only herself, but Ann as well.

She dropped instantly to the ground and tried to signal but Ann was not looking. She was sitting on a log with her head in her hands. Impossible to shout a warning; a shout would carry far down the valley. Mary began to run. If only she could move fast enough to keep ahead of whoever was coming up the creekbed! If only she and Ann could reach home unnoticed! She ran frantically down the slope, across the bottom of the ravine and up the other side, spilling acorns as she went.

At last Ann lifted her head and saw her. Mary stopped just long enough to point behind her and then ran on. Now Ann too saw the startled birds and recognized them as a sign of danger. Had they time to reach the house? She grabbed Mary's hand as she came panting up the slope and together they fled towards home.

They made it at last, falling white-faced and breathless through the door. Their mother and sisters knew from their frightened faces that danger must be close on their heels. Catherine dashed out and dragged the little boys into the house, shutting the door and latching it behind her. Sarah, an expert marksman at seventeen, reached for the musket on the wall and shouldered it.

They all held their breath as they waited in silence, waited – and waited. A squirrel scolded angrily nearby, a bluejay screamed, a stick cracked, and there was the sound of pebbles scrunched underfoot. They looked at each other enquiringly. Surely no Indian would make all that noise. They heard footsteps and men's voices and then a sharp rap on the door.

"Who's there?" called Mrs. Whitmore.

"Bill Sheets" came the answer. "Is this the Whitmore cabin?"

"Yes," answered Mrs. Whitmore, throwing open the door. Before her stood, not Indians but two white men - strangers - roughly dressed in hunting clothes.

Sarah put the musket back on its rack.

"Bill Sheets" said her mother. "Could you be, could you – possibly be my brother Jacob's son?"

"Yes, that's who I am and this is my friend Henry Hoople. We have come all the way from the Mohawk Valley in the Colony of New York to see my father's sister."

The family stood around, amazed, while their mother hugged her nephew and welcomed his friend.

Mary and Ann were red-faced now feeling somewhat abashed about their headlong flight from a danger that did not exist. Mary felt guilty too for she had known all along that it was wrong to cross the ravine.

Repentant or not Mary was never one to remain downhearted for long. Her blue eyes sparkled as she leaned close to Ann and whispered, "Isn't he handsome?"

"Who, our cousin?"

"No, no, the other one."

Chapter 2

ON CHILLISQUAQUE CREEK

Mary wriggled her bare toes under the table as she looked into the laughing blue eyes of the stranger. Never before had she seen such an expression of fun and kindness. Ignoring a sharp kick from Sarah, a kick that plainly meant, "Get up and help me to serve this mush," she continued to gaze fascinated at the visitors.

Her cousin Bill was describing the long journey that had brought him and Henry from the Mohawk country in New York to this pioneer cabin on Chillisquaque Creek, which in 1779 was still the frontier forest of Pennsylvania.

"It was easy," said Bill, "down river all the way so we didn't have to paddle much and there was little portaging to do. The East Branch of the Susquehanna rises in Otsego Lake not far from Henry's farm. We came down it past Unadilla and Tioga, both in ruins since Sullivan's expedition this summer against the Senecas. We came through Wyoming, wrecked by Walter Butler and our British Indians last year, and on through Fishing Creek to Shamokin."

"Could you live off the land?" asked Phillip, the eldest of the Whitmores.

"Yes, but not well. There was little game left after Sullivan's 10,000 men went up river in July. We caught some fish, but lived mostly on rabbits and racoons with an occasional beaver."

"How long did it take you?" questioned Jake.

"About ten days," answered Henry, as he turned his attention from Mary to Jake. "It will take three times that long to get home paddling upstream against the current."

"And how did you know where to find us?" asked Mr. Whitmore.

"We asked the Rangers at Fort Augusta in Shamokin and they directed us. They said they knew you, that you came out twice a year for supplies and ammunition. 'Go up the West Branch of the Susquehanna, to the first creek on your right that empties into it. That will be Chillisquaque or Frozen Duck Creek. Follow it to its source and you will find the Whitmore cabin there beside a spring in a pleasant valley'."

"My father sent us," continued Bill. "Aunt," he said, turning to Mrs. Whitmore, "Father claims you were always his favourite sister and he hates to think of you way out here in this exposed position in such perilous times. He thinks you would be safer to come back with us to the Mohawk where the women and children would have others for company in the stone forts there, and Mr. Whitmore and Phillip, maybe even Jake, could join the King's forces. Father is already in Sir John Johnson's regiment, The Royal Greens, and Henry and I plan to enlist too when we get back home."

"I do not want to fight," answered Peter Whitmore. "I prefer to farm. King George needs troops, but he also needs farmers to grow food for his troops. Besides, we are not in any danger. The Indians around here are our friends. This was Delaware country and they know that we paid a fair price for our land. They are not likely to harm us. As to their overlords, the Senecas, they fight for the British and they know that I am a King's man. Who else is there in these parts? Only a few Oneidas who are neutral."

"Supposed to be neutral, you mean," interrupted Phillip. "Some of them are fighting for the Revolution in Washington's armies."

"Some of the Senecas are too," added Bill.

"And what about De Coignée?" put in Jake. "You said yourself that you could not trust that weasel."

"True. De Coignée is treacherous - a disgrace to both his French and Indian blood. He fights first for one side and then the other. I am sure he would stick a knife in my back as soon as look at me, if it suited his purpose. But then he is an exception. The others I trust. We have good neighbours here too who came with us from New Jersey. You probably noticed the smoke from their chimneys as you came up the valley."

"Yes, we saw two columns of smoke rising in the distance to the east."

"The one on your left was from Daniel Welliver's home on Whetsone Run which flows into Little Fishing Creek. The other was from Michael Billhime's cabin on Muddy Run."

At this point Mrs. Whitmore, who had been nursing the baby, broke in, "But Peter they are leaving, going home to New Jersey, and then we will be all alone. Maybe my brother Jacob is right when he says we are too exposed here on the frontier."

"Wife, I told you before that I am not going to move. I put all I had into this land and five years hard work as well, and here I stay."

"But Father, if everyone says it is not safe . . .".

"NO", roared Peter Whitmore, bringing his fist down on the table with such force that all the wooden bowls and pewter spoons leapt into the air and down again with a great clatter. He then stood up, ending the discussion and the meal.

"Water, Mary," said Sarah, firmly handing her sister the wooden bucket. This time Mary knew better than to neglect her chores. She grabbed the bucket and scurried out the door towards the spring, hoping to get the job done quickly so she could return and enjoy the company of the visitors.

She had not gone far when she heard footsteps behind her and Henry's deep voice saying, "Here, give me that. It's hot in the cabin," as he went with her to the spring. Overhead the stars were sparkling in the cold autumn sky, the air was sweet with the scent of birch burning on the cabin hearth and, far in the distance, they heard the eerie barking of a fox.

Hardly had they reached the door with the water when six year old George came running to Mary for help. "Polly," he said using her nickname, "I cut my knee on the scythe." He had indeed. Blood was spurting from the gash and, as was the custom in their family, he turned to Mary when first aid was needed.

By the time George's knee was bandaged and the wooden bowls washed and turned upside down to drip, Mr. Whitmore had collected the guests and his family of ten around the hearth for their regular evening prayer service. He sat in the centre on a stool with an English Bible open on one knee and a copy of the German hymn book, the Marsburger Gesangbuch, on the other. This last had been brought to America nearly a hundred years before by one of his wife's Lutheran ancestors.

Near the chimney of field-stone and mud sat Mrs. Whitmore, rocking the cradle with her toe. Her three eldest daughters sat on the floor at her knee. Opposite them on a log Phillip was trying out hymn tunes on his home-made flute, while Jake and the little boys squatted cross-legged beside him.

"Which is it to be tonight?" asked their father as Mary took her place in the circle.

"Ein feste Burg," shouted everyone in unison.

Phillip tuned up for Martin Luther's famous hymn, "A Safe Stronghold Our God Is Still" and they all sang lustily in German.

"Now," announced Mr. Whitmore, "I will read my favourite psalm, the twenty-third. He read it slowly in English. There really was no need. His children had heard it so often they could recite it word for word from memory in either English or German or, as more often happened, in a mixture of the two.

"My people," said their father, "came from England. They fought under Cromwell and when he died and Charles II became King of England they had to flee for their lives to Holland. There they stayed for about sixty years until some of them decided to try their fortunes in America and sailed from Amsterdam to New York. It was a long rough passage, and in one bad storm that rocked the ship from bow to stern the frightened immigrants huddled below decks in the stuffy hold, expecting every moment to be their last. Those terrified people were comforted and calmed when my father recited to them the twenty-third psalm ending with these words: 'Yea, though I walk through the valley of the shadow of death I will fear no evil for Thou art with me'."

That night the big boys slept on the floor in order

to give their bunk to the visitors. In the morning everyone was up early to see the guests off. Mrs. Whitmore had baked hominy cakes for them to take with them, and she busily gathered together other food for their journey.

Outside the cabin Henry came upon Mary sitting on a stump drawing on birchbark with a charred stick. Her head was bent above the sketch so that her two braids hung loosely over her shoulders. She was flushed with the effort she was making. The little boys stood admiringly around her.

"That's our house," said Peter, "with mother in the doorway holding the baby."

"And that's me right there," said Johnny, pointing with a pudgy finger, "and that's Mary with the bucket going to the spring."

"Yes, I can see that," said Henry. "It is good, very good."

"Here, if you like it take it to remember us by," and Mary gave the birchbark to him.

"Thanks, thanks a lot."

Chapter 3

THE LONG WINTER

An uneasy gloom descended on the Whitmore household after the visitors departed and the last golden leaves of October had drifted to earth leaving the trees stark and bare in the forest.

One day their neighbour, Daniel Welliver appeared at the door "We are leaving tomorrow. I wish you would change your mind and come with us."

"No," said Peter Whitmore, "I don't believe in changing my mind once it is made up."

"Very well then, be it on your own head. My wife says if that is the case she wants you all to come to our place this evening for a farewell shindig."

The party was gay only on the surface since Mary, and in fact everyone in the three families, was depressed at the thought of the coming separation. Her brother Phillip was particularly blue for he was devoted to Betsy Billhime. Usually at these parties he played for the square dances on his reed flute but this time he persuaded one of the Billhime boys to spell him off. He went through one reel with Betsy as partner and then the two of them disappeared, and Mary saw them sitting together in the shadows at the edge of the clearing.

When the dancers were tired they gathered around a campfire to eat venison stew and sing all their favourite songs. Finally the moon rose high over the hills and it was time to say goodbye.

In the morning no friendly columns of smoke to the eastward greeted their eyes as they opened the cabin door. Mary noticed the sad look on her mother's face and went to stand close to her as a gesture of comfort.

"I am not complaining," said her mother, "only it seems so lonesome. For five years they have been our close friends, our only neighbours."

"Maybe the war will end soon and they will come back," offered Mary hopefully.

"Maybe," and a little sigh accompanied the word.

Jake went over to the Wellivers as he had always done and came home crestfallen. "They have really gone," he said. "Both houses are closed and empty."

"Naturally," replied Phillip, "what else did you expect? They said last night they were going."

"Well, I thought they might have changed their minds."

"Some people never change their minds," answered Phillip bitterly, with a meaning glance at his father.

His mother hastily changed the subject to avert trouble. "Do go, Phil, and see how much salt we have. I suspect there may not be enough left to put down our winter supply of fish."

Mr. Whitmore and Jake departed for the day to cut wood in the bush, and Mary went to the spring for water. When she returned her mother and Phillip were talking earnestly in low voices. They did not see her come in and she could not help overhearing what they said.

"If Father had not been so stubborn we could have gone with them to New Jersey and then Betsy and I could have been married at Christmas."

"Try not to be so critical of your father, Phillip. What he did was for your sake, for you and the other boys. He had good reasons for staying here. We own this property but in New Jersey we would own nothing. You and your father and Jake would have to hire out there for a few cents a day and how then could you afford to marry Betsy? And, there is another point; it is not certain that it is any safer there than here. That dreadful Minisink Massacre a couple of years ago took place close to our old home in New Jersey."

"Well anyway, Betsy has promised to wait for me and I'm going for her in the spring as soon as our seeding is finished."

"You are a grown man, son. You must decide for yourself. I'm glad you plan to see your father through the spring work first. He badly needs your help. He carries a great burden of responsibility, having to make life and death decisions for his children and then ever afterwards having to wonder if they were really for the best."

A long lonely winter lay ahead. Preparations for Christmas provided the only gaiety in their lives as the drab and dreary days of November and early December passed slowly by. Jake arranged a stick calendar on the wall so they could keep track of the dates, a new stick each month, a new notch each night to show another day gone. "Twenty more days to Christmas – fifteen more days to Christmas."

They made gifts out of whatever materials they found at hand. The girls had collected everlasting flowers in the summer and they dyed these now with herbs and berries to make a bouquet for their mother. The boys

24

whittled knitting needles out of ironwood sticks and Mary took the little children on snowshoes into the bush to gather strands of the shiny dark green pipsissewa vine, showing them how to twist these into wreaths decorated with red bunch berries for a gift to their parents.

Mr. Whitmore had already shot two wild turkeys and preserved them frozen on the cabin roof for the special yuletide feast. His wife stuffed these and roasted them on a spit in the open hearth on Christmas morning, and the tantalizing smell filled the house.

Once Christmas was past the short days and long cold nights of January seemed to stretch endlessly before them.

Mary hardly knew whether she was a child or a woman. Sometimes she acted like one; sometimes like the other. On very cold bright days when the invigorating air was crystal clear and the snow sparkled in the sunshine she would join her little brothers on the slide and shriek with joy as she sped sideways down its icy slope. At other times, feeling quite grown up and dignified, she sat with her mother and the big girls around the hearth making new clothes or mending old ones.

The girls begged their mother to tell them stories of the olden times while they sewed. Their favourite was about the crazy patchwork quilt that adorned their mother's bed. They could look at it there on the bunk while she talked, admiring its uneven shapes of red and yellow, purple, green and blue which stood out vividly against the plain brown walls of the log cabin.

"It was my wedding present," she would begin, "My mother arranged a surprise quilting bee. Friends and neighbours came bringing with them whatever pieces they had of coloured cloth; wool, linen or linsey-woolsey. Before the party was over there was my wedding quilt all sewn together and quilted."

Once she told them about the great uncle who had lost his life on the frontiers of Virginia.

"It happened a long time ago. One of my Sheets uncles and his wife and children with another couple named Taylor left New Jersey to homestead in Virginia. At that time there was great unrest among the Indians, who naturally enough resented the white people taking their hunting lands away from them. This resulted in border warfare with constant raids and massacres.

"The Sheets and Taylors had a horse and wagon, so when a runner came by warning everyone that hostile Indians had been seen in the vicinity the two men put their wives and children into the wagon and set out through the woods for the nearest fort.

"Half way there they were attacked by five Indians who tomahawked both the men and then turned on the women. One Indian grabbed a Sheets child by the arm to drag him out of the wagon, but the mother was too quick for him. She held her boy by his other arm and, seizing the axe from her dead husband's hand she hit that Indian such a blow on the skull that he had to let go of the child and stagger off into the bush. Meantime, Mrs. Taylor had taken her dead husband's axe and was fighting too. In the end those Indians were so sorely wounded that the five of them skulked off out of sight and the women and children were able to continue to the fort."

There was complete silence around the fireplace as the girls thought about the story.

"Mother, how far is it to Shamokin?"

"About sixteen miles."

"Could we make it there if we were attacked?"

"I doubt it. Indians could slip through the bush quicker than we could and ambush us somewhere on the way. That is why people call our situation here 'exposed'."

Another silence followed, broken only by the crackling of the wood on the hearth. Then Catherine sniffed loudly and a tear dropped on the pants she was patching. "I don't like such sad stories. They frighten me."

"The ending of that story is not really sad," replied Mrs. Whitmore. "Because of the bravery of those mothers their youngsters were saved to grow up and marry and have children of their own. Now, so folks say, the Shenandoah Valley in Virginia is peopled with families by the names of Sheets and Taylor."

One night not long after this Mary woke with a start. She felt sure that some dreaded sound had wakened her but she could not think what it was. She lay very still listening. At first all she heard was the cracking and booming of the great trees in the forest protesting against the bitter cold. Then she heard the sound again, the hoarse, frightening cough of a baby with the croup.

Her mother was already up with the baby in her arms when Mary jumped out of bed. "Good girl," she said. "Get the onions and put them in the fire."

Mary knelt shivering in front of the hearth, poking onions into the center of the hot hardwood coals that had been banked with ashes to keep them alive through the night. As soon as the onions were roasted she held the croaking baby while her mother prepared the juice and fed it in large doses to the child, at the same time placing an onion poultice on its chest. However, the hoarse cough continued. The poor little mite could hardly breathe.

Mary watched anxiously. "I was staying at the Billhimes when their baby died of the croup."

"I know, dear, but Mrs. Billhime did not listen to me. She left it too late in starting the onion cure. We should be able to catch this in time."

"I surely hope so." Mary hated to see her baby sister struggle so hard to get breath and the coughs she noticed were becoming worse not better.

"Mary, come here!" The command was low and urgent. "Come and help me pray." Frightened, Mary and her mother looked at each other for a second above the tiny frame. Then Mrs. Whitmore closed her eyes and whispered, "Dear God, if it pleases you, spare this child."

"Amen," said Mary.

No sound broke the quiet of the cold, dark cabin

for some time after that except the regular breathing of the sleeping family. Then the baby coughed again, a softer sound. From then on there were longer and longer intervals between the spasms until the coughing gradually faded away.

"Thank you, Lord," said Mrs. Whitmore. She looked earnestly at Mary. "Listen to me," she said. "I want to tell you something very important. If anything terrible happens – to us here, or you are alone and in trouble – always remember that God loves you and has the power to help you. Ask and trust. Help will come even though you may not get it in the way you expect."

Eventually, when February gave way to March, Mary saw crows flying north and sensed the stirring of a new exciting feeling in the sunshine. Spring was certainly in the air with the warm days and frosty nights that were just right for sugaring off.

"Sap's running," Jake burst out joyously. "This year it's my turn to tend the fires in the Sugar Bush, with Catherine and Ann to keep me company."

His father looked grave. "That's impossible, Son. I hardly feel it is safe for you young folks out there alone in these uncertain times."

"But, Father, you promised! It is our turn. Phillip did it last year with Sarah and Mary, and you promised – remember?"

Yes, Peter Whitmore remembered his promise and wished he had not made it. Never in all his life had he allowed himself to break a promise. Reluctant though he now was, he gave his permission. Jake and the two girls left with blanket rolls and everything needed to sleep in the open. The rest of the family planned to join them in the morning.

As Mary climbed into bed she sensed anxiety and tension in her mother. From her own bunk, where she lay with one arm around little Johnny, she could see a corner of the patchwork quilt hanging loosely over the side of her parents' bunk. She was gazing at it drowsily when she heard her mother speak.

"Peter, I wish we had not let them go. I am afraid. I have a terrible feeling that there is danger near us. I sense danger all around us."

There was an inaudible mumble from her father and then she heard her mother's voice again, praying out loud.

"God, please, if it be Your will, keep Jake, Catherine and Ann safe in the Sugar Bush."

In the silence that followed Mary dropped off into a troubled sleep.

Chapter 4

THE MASSACRE

The blood-curdling war cry that roused the household in the pre-dawn hours paralyzed Mary with fright. She opened her eyes on a scene of horror that was to be imprinted on her mind forever.

Phillip was kneeling by the hearth trying to start the fire. Behind him in the open doorway stood a Seneca chief in full war paint, his tomahawk raised for the fatal blow. Over the man's shoulder she glimpsed the sinister face of De Coignée, his musket at his shoulder ready to shoot, and beyond him others: Senecas, Delawares, Oneidas and a few ruffian whites from the Revolutionary Army, all armed and making threatening noises.

Her father leapt from bed and reached for his musket but at the same moment a shot from De Coignée laid him out dead on the floor. The first Indian buried his hatchet in Phillip's head and a second did the same to Mrs. Whitmore, grabbing her by her long hair and scalping her. Sarah caught the baby as it fell from her mother's arms and rushed outside. Mary clutched Johnny by the hand and followed, as did their brothers Peter and George. They ran madly for the woods. It was no use. They were all caught instantly, flung on horses and held there by Indian guards.

By this time the house had been looted and set ablaze. As it burst into flames the whole raiding party sprang onto the horses and rode off to the westward in frantic haste.

At the sudden lunging motion of the horse the frightened baby in Sarah's arms began to scream, its thin piercing wail cutting through the air like a knife. Sarah tried in vain to hush it, then the Indian who held her wrenched the screaming child from her arms and, holding it by one foot, swung it around his head and dashed its brains out against the nearest tree leaving the little body where it fell.

Both Sarah and Mary screamed and struggled to get off the horses to go to the baby, but Sarah's Indian clobbered her and Mary's dug a knife into her ribs so that she felt blood on her clothes and she dared not struggle any more. Their captors made it clear that the same thing would happen to them if they did not keep quiet, for the marauders feared a rescue party would hear and give them chase. The roar of the flames enveloping the cabin and the thick clouds of smoke that came from it were soon left far behind as the steady pounding of horse hoofs carried them westward into an unfamiliar section of the forest.

The shock, grief, horror and fear she felt were too much for Mary to bear and in spite of efforts to restrain herself she was obliged to lean over the horse's neck and be sick. The stern-faced Indian who held her paid no heed. To add to her miseries she was now caught between two bad smells, the unpleasant odour she had just created herself and the unbearable stench of the rancid bear's grease with which her captor had coated himself.

On and on they went down deep ravines and up steep mountain trails. From the top of one peak, looking back, Mary saw the smoke from the cabin still rising into the sky but now it was a long way off. How far they must have come already! Would a rescue party ever catch up? Ever find them? She thought of Jake and the two girls in the Sugar Bush. Had they been spared perhaps to give the alarm and raise a rescue party? And where would they find any settlers that they could rouse in time? Shamokin, as her mother had said, was sixteen miles away. "Mother, oh Mother," sobbed Mary.

It comforted her a little to see Sarah on the horse ahead. Once when the trail made a sharp turn to the right she caught a glimpse of something red through the bare branches of the trees and realized that it must be Johnny's sweater. "Poor little Johnny," she thought. "I will have to be a mother to him now." It was a sad thought but it brought a shred of comfort with it for it gave her a purpose in living.

Hour after hour the relentless hoof beats carried them farther away from the place that had been their happy home. The sun came up behind them to eastward, rose above their heads at noon and sank gradually beyond the mountain tops to the west, but the pace never slackened. There was no rest and no food all that day.

After dark the cavalcade stopped in a deep ravine beside an unknown river and the captives were set on the ground. They were forced to walk about to bring the circulation back to their feet. Each of them was then given a couple of handfuls of crushed corn that seemed sweet to the taste and a gourd of water from the river to wash it down. While they ate this meagre fare their captors guarded them by forming a tight ring around them. De Coignée and the white ruffians were no longer among them. Mary noticed that her Indian, whom she had come to think of as Stern One, was washing his horse's mane in the river and she was thankful. In about twenty minutes they took again to the trail and rode all that night.

With the coming of dawn the snowy crests of the mountains before them took on a warm, rosy glow, while the nearest hills and deep valleys between appeared purple and dark blue changing to mauve and turquoise as the sun climbed higher in the sky. They rode on through those seemingly endless mountains all the second day without stopping, and at long last Mary began to realize that hope of a rescue party was now out of the question.

The same thought must have been in the minds of their captors for they relaxed somewhat on the second night in an open glade surrounded by dark green spruce trees. Again the prisoners were made to walk and were fed the same rations as before. Evergreen boughs were laid on the snowy ground and the captives, although carefully watched on all sides, were allowed to lie down together in a row on this rough bed.

Mary was glad of the warmth of Johnny's little body in front of her and Sarah's at her back. Utterly exhausted she was just sinking into a deep sleep when she heard Sarah whispering in her ear. She spoke in German which she thought their guards would not be able to understand as readily as English. "I'm afraid they will separate us," she said. "I have heard that Indians often divide up their prisoners. If they do, never forget your name or Father's name and where you came from."

"I could never forget that, Sally,"

"Yes, you could. I've heard of captured children who learned the Indian language and forgot their own tongue and their own names so that when white people at last found them no one knew who they were. I don't want that to happen to any of us. Remember, learn it by heart, repeat it every day until you are rescued. – 'My name is Mary Whitmore and I was born in New Jersey. My father's name was Peter and he was killed near Shamokin in Pennsylvania on Easter Day in 1780.' Promise me Mary to do that."

"I promise. Listen Sarah I think mother knew something dreadful was going to happen. One day she warned me. She said, 'If anything terrible happens remember that God loves you and will help you if you ask Him.' Sally, I can't understand why He didn't help mother and father. Can you?"

"Perhaps He did, Polly. They are safe with Him now."

Sarah's voice went on whispering but Mary could not stay awake to listen. The last thing she heard her say was "Do what they tell you and they will be kind to you."

Mary woke a few hours later while it was still dark.

She felt the warmth of Johnny in front of her but nothing except a cold blast of air was at her back. She turned to look. Sarah was not there, neither were Peter or George. On the spot where they had been sleeping crouched a wide-awake Indian guard, his shiny black eyes on her, his loaded musket slung across his knee.

Mary was so desperate she didn't care what she did. She opened her mouth and screamed at the top of her lungs, "Sarah, Sarah where is my sister Sarah?" Instantly the entire camp was on its feet. Stern One came over and shook her angrily, motioning her to be quiet but Mary was beyond caring. She was hysterical with grief and fear, and screamed again, "Sarah where are you?"

"Gone," said Stern One. He raised one arm dramatically and pointed to the hills. "Gone, Senecas, one white girl, two white boys – gone." He used his fingers to indicate the words "One and Two".

Mary fell in a heap against Johnny sobbing her heart out in despair. Sarah had been right about the Indians separating their prisoners and now she would never see her again. Why hadn't she stayed awake last night and listened to her sister while she was still with her. "Johnny, darling," she sobbed. "They are gone. Sally and Pete and George are GONE!"

"Where?" demanded Johnny looking straight at the Indian in front of him.

"Senecas."

"Where are we going?" Johnny made it plain what 'we' meant by pointing to Mary and himself.

To Mary's amazement Stern One apparently understood the question and answered it in his own language. "Lenni Lenape Allegwinenk." he said.

Mary recognized "Lenni Lenape" as the name the

Delaware used to describe themselves and it was easy to guess from the sound of it that "Allegwinenk" meant the Allegheny River Country to which some of the tribe had moved when their lands in Pennsylvania were taken over by white settlers.

Looking around her now she could see that there were no Senecas or Oneidas in sight. The nine braves who remained, all strangers to her, were the very ones whom she had previously guessed to be Delawares. There was a certain physical likeness among them and their war paint was similar, red or black on their faces with a white streak under each eye.

Stern One now knelt on one knee in front of Johnny and a gentle expression of pleasure and admiration replaced the usually grim look on his face. "My brother," he said solemnly in a low guttural tone, placing a hand on the little boy's shoulder.

"My brother," corrected Mary.

"No." Stern One pointed across the glade to a young warrior busily unhitching his horse. "Long Arrow your brother. White Boy my brother."

"Aha," thought Mary, "so that is the plan. Johnny and I are to be adopted into different families. I only hope they do not separate us into different villages as well."

Soon they were again on the trail westward. That day as they rode the mountains gave way to rolling hills, the forest became less dense with more oaks and poplars and fewer of the dark towering pines and dainty white birch trees that had been a familiar sight in the forest around Mary's home. How, she wondered, could she and Johnny escape? And if they did, could they find their way back through the maze of mountains to – to what? Their home was burned, their parents dead, the rest of their family murdered or scattered. It seemed hopeless, useless, to dream of escape, yet Mary could think of nothing else.

In the light covering of snow on the ground tracks of various animals showed clearly. They passed deer, rabbit, racoon and occasionally bear tracks. None of these seemed to interest their captors so Mary was surprised when the horsemen ahead of her stopped and dismounted to examine carefully and discuss at some length a trail through the snow. Stern One did not dismount. He edged his horse sideways until he, and of course Mary also, could see over the heads of the other Indians. These were panther tracks of an immense size. To Mary they looked exactly like those of her cat at home only a great many times larger.

They got on their way again but with a difference. The panther tracks helped Mary to change her mind about wanting to escape. "What," she thought, "could Johnny and I do alone and on foot in the forest, if we met a bear or a panther on the trail?" She decided right then and there, with the practical commonsense mind that she had inherited from her mother's people, to be thankful that they had horses to ride and Indian guards who knew the way to lead them and feed them. After all, she thought, these Indians are human beings and much safer to be with than the wild beasts — that is provided they do not torture us when they get us home.

Chapter 5

DELAWARE ENCAMPMENT

By sunrise on the fourth morning everything had changed. Mary woke up in an open space near a small hill covered with hickory trees. She and Johnny were completely ignored. No one bothered to feed them or guard them so they sat together on a fallen log and watched with amazement as the Indians, in pairs, helped each other apply fresh war paint to their features. Mary shuddered, wondering if they were preparing to go out again on the warpath.

"What is that noise?" she said to Johnny.

"Drums. They are coming to welcome us."

He was right. The fresh war paint was for the triumphal procession into the Delawares' home village - just over the hill.

When they were ready each brave leapt on his horse brandishing in one hand whatever article of loot he had brought back from the Whitmore cabin. It was easy to see what they valued most - the copper kettle, their father's musket and, proudly displayed across his horse's back by one of the older braves, their mother's many-coloured patchwork quilt.

Stern One now approached, placed a string of wampum beadwork around each of their necks, then took Johnny by the hand and put him on his own horse at the head of the procession. In the same way Long Arrow came over to Mary and took her to his horse, as if it were his right to lead her captive to his home.

The drums were louder now. It was time to start. Up and over the hill they went, the horses stepping with slow dignity as if they sensed the importance of the occasion. As they topped the rise all the warriors shot their guns off into the air and this volley was answered by a similar salvo from the camp below them.

When the smoke cleared Mary saw laid out before her on a flat plain encircled on three sides by hills and on the fourth by a river, a village of about twenty bark wigwams each one small and circular in shape with a slightly peaked roof from which rose a spiral of smoke. In the centre of these, looking expectantly towards the oncoming procession stood a motley crowd of old men, women and children.

So, thought Mary her heart sinking, this is to be our new home. Perhaps it will be better than being lost in the bitter cold of the mountains or being eaten alive by wild beasts. I only hope they do not plan to torture us. "Dear God", she whispered, "please do not let them torture us." She watched anxiously for any sign of the women forming into two long lines with clubs to make them run the gauntlet.

No such thing took place.

Instead, the crowd broke up into what seemed to be small family groups, which surrounded the brave or braves belonging to them, and led them triumphantly to their own dwellings.

Those who welcomed Long Arrow were an old woman, two young women, a very beautiful girl about Mary's own age and several small children. The old warrior who was displaying her mother's quilt was also welcomed by this group.

Long Arrow jumped from his horse and, lifting Mary down, presented her with a great show of pride to the older woman. At the same time the old man handed over to her the patchwork quilt and they moved towards the nearest wigwam.

Mary cast a quick look over her shoulder to see what was happening to Johnny. She was just able to catch a glimpse of his red sweater disappearing into an extra large lodge on the far side of the clearing before she herself was propelled inside the nearest dwelling through a flapping skin doorway.

The place was blue with smoke from a central campfire and the air inside stale with many odours, but Mary noticed none of this. Her eyes, her whole mind and body were rivetted on the fact that a large pot of venison stew hung from a crane over the fire and to her starving, empty stomach the smell of it was overpowering.

Exhausted by shock and grief, weak from lack of food, tired out with three days on the trail, it was little wonder that her self-control gave way. Her eyes filled with tears and her knees shook beneath her as she stood there waiting silently inside the doorflap. Then the old woman led her to the fire and placed in her hands a wooden bowl of stew, after which she treated the two men in the same way.

There was only one spoon, a large wooden one for ladling but Mary did not care or even notice. She picked chunks of deer-meat out of the bowl with her fingers as the men were doing, and slurped down great gulps of the tasty soup.

The rest of the family were busily examining the quilt but the young girl broke away from them and going over to Mary knelt down with her beside the fire. Before long the heat and the food coming after so much exposure caused Mary's eyes to close and her head to droop. The girl helped her to her feet, and, indicating one of the bunks built around the wall, waved a hand for her to climb in.

The bed was made of saplings raised a few feet from the ground and partitioned off at either end from the next bunk. It had a strong sapling roof, obviously used for storage purposes, and was furnished with two large bearskins. Mary needed no second invitation. She crawled in between the bearskins and fell fast asleep.

Many hours later she was wakened by the rhythmic beat of drums punctuated by terrifying war cries. A torture ceremony perhaps? And what of Johnny? Her heart was in her mouth as she sprang out of bed in the dark and, groping her way to the doorflap, stepped outside.

She was transfixed by the scene that met her eyes. The whole centre of the village was lit up by a campfire around which danced the Delaware braves in full war paint and ceremonial dress, brandishing tomahawks over their heads, stamping so heavily that the very ground shook, and leaping wildly in the air with each war-whoop.

In the darkness beyond the fire was a ring of spectators and Mary strained her eyes to catch a glimpse of Johnny among them. Suddenly she spotted his red sweater - not among the spectators at all but bobbing up and down with the dancers. He was stomping with his short stubby legs 'thump thump' on the right foot 'thump thump' on the left, and in his hand he brandished a stick for a tomahawk as he followed directly behind Stern One, imitating his every move.

The horror of the scene sickened Mary as she realized that this was no torture ceremony but a victory dance - and the victory they were celebrating - that Johnny was helping to celebrate - was the massacre of their parents, their brother Phillip and their baby sister. She sank down in a heap beside the wigwam and, closing her eyes to shut out the hideous sight, covered her ears with her hands.

After a while she felt a soft bump and opened her eyes to find Johnny leaning against her and looking up into her face. "Polly, I did it. I danced like a Delaware warrior. Did you see me?"

"Yes, I saw you."

She struggled to keep back the words of horror, resisting a desire to tell him the terrible meaning of the dance and to scold him for taking part in it.

"What is the matter, Polly? Didn't I dance well?"

Years later Mary was to remember that moment as the one in which she changed from a child to a woman, as the moment when she overcame her own feelings of horror in order to sympathize with a little boy's pride in what, to him, was an innocent accomplishment.

"Yes, darling," she said, "you danced wonderfully." Then to distract him she took him into the wigwam to show him her bed. He was not impressed.

"Our house is much bigger," he boasted. "It is the biggest one of all 'cause Stern One is a sort of chief' - did you know that Polly? And his name is not Stern One. It is Bear Claw. He is the captain of this village and I am to be his adopted brother so I may be a captain or a chief too some day."

Mary led him outside again still chattering, and

they sat down in the shadows where Johnny, exhausted by his efforts in the dance, fell asleep against her knee. When a woman came to claim him and carry him off to the big wigwam across the way Mary did not protest. She felt it might be safer for Johnny to let him go along with whatever plans they had for him, for she remembered Sarah's last whispered instruction, "Do as they tell you and they will be kind to you."

The women of Long Arrow's family soon went to bed but the men kept on dancing to the drums in the fire-light the whole night through. Mary lay sleepless between the bearskins, gazing at the patchwork quilt where they had hung it inside the doorflap. Its colours glowed in the flickering light from the banked campfire and recalled to her the sound of her mother's voice and the last words she had ever heard her say, "God please keep Jake and Catherine and Ann safe." Where they safe? Were they perhaps alive even now - somewhere miles away on the other side of the mountains?

Mary determined to find out if they had been spared, and for this purpose she decided to learn to speak and understand the Delaware language as soon as she could.

A cold blast of air from the opening doorflap hit Mary across the face as Johnny entered and hurled himself on to her bunk.

"Take me in, Polly," he sobbed, "I'se so lonesome."

Another cold blast and over Johnny's head Mary saw that the woman from the big wigwam had come in search of her charge. Long Arrow's mother got up and greeted her, apparently persuading her to leave Johnny alone. The two women chuckled together for a few minutes and then the stranger left.

Mary hugged Johnny to her and pondered the new things she had just learned about Indian women; that they could laugh at the antics of children and that their hearts were warm enough to let a small homesick boy spend the night with his sister.

Johnny was gone when Mary woke next morning. The two men exhausted by their night-long dancing were snoring heavily but apart from them the house was empty - not a woman or child in sight. She rescued one of the wooden bowls from the dogs, and took it outside and washed it with snow, helped herself to some soup from the kettle and then set forth to explore the village. This appeared to be deserted except for the unfettered horses which were nibbling grass on the fringes of the clearing between patches of melting snow.

There was the sound of childish laughter some-where in the distance near the river and she went to investigate. There she found Johnny throwing snowballs at a distant tree trunk in competition with several other boys.

"Watch me, Polly. See how far I can throw."

It was the same old story of little boys wanting an audience. Even the Indian children, although they pre-tended not to notice her, glanced at her sideways with their shiny eyes as if to say, "Watch this one, watch me." It was exactly the way Peter and George had always behaved at home.

The young girl from Long Arrow's family now appeared among the trees on the brow of a nearby hill and beckoned to Mary to come with her. Together they followed a trail for some distance into the bush.

Mary pointing to herself said "Mary". The girl

pointed to herself and said some unpronounceable Delaware word, then, seeing Mary's puzzlement, she stooped and drew an antlered buck in the snow with a small doe beside it. This last, she explained in sign language, was her name. Mary understood her to mean that her name was "Little Doe", one that suited her perfectly with her big soft eyes and gentle ways.

The path led them to a maple grove where they found all the women busily dismantling the camp. Sugaring was over for the season. Little Doe took Mary to the one remaining fire where a kettle of sap was still bubbling and motioned for her to stir it with a wooden paddle. This seemed strange. At home she had been trained never to stir sap at this stage for fear it would crystalize into powder instead of hardening into cakes. However, the girl was firm so Mary shrugged and obeyed.

Little Doe produced baskets filled with small skin bags that looked oddly familiar. Soon the sap turned to powder and the Indian girl added some of it to each little bag already partially filled with cornmeal, shook it well and tied it up with hempen cord. Now Mary knew why the little bags looked familiar - they were similar to those from which the braves on the trail westward had fed their prisoners sweetened cornmeal. They must have been prepared ahead of time like these, which were no doubt next year's supply of food pouches for Long Arrow and the old man to take with them on the warpath.

The girls put out the fire and carried the bags home, hanging them carefully on storage pegs in the wigwam well above the reach of children and dogs.

It was a sunny day. What snow remained was fast melting and the women now sat outside their homes pounding cornmeal in hollowed stumps with wooden pestles. This was a task to which Mary was well accustomed. She grabbed a pestle and brought it down in a businesslike manner on the hard kernels of corn, giving it a circular twist as she did so. The old woman of her new family made approving noises in her throat and Mary was glad to have something familiar and useful to do.

As she worked she noticed several men in the centre of the campsite who appeared to be puzzling over something in their hands. They turned it this way and that and shook their heads as if they had no idea what it was. Mary was amused when she saw that it was her mother's little handmill.

Her father had bought the new-fangled gadget at Shamokin for thirteen beaver skins and brought it home to ease his wife's constant toil of grinding corn. Mrs. Whitmore, however, had soon discovered that it was harder to work and less efficient than the simple stump.

As Mary watched the men she fought a silent battle within herself against the bitterness she felt towards them. Could she forgive them for the murder of her parents and help them or not? She decided to let go of the bitterness, reasoning that after all these were not the men who had done the actual killing – that had been De Coignée and the Senecas. These men had been kind to her and Johnny.

She filled a bark vessel with corn kernels and going over to the men held out her hand for the mill. Surprised they let her have it and stood back to watch as she poured the corn into it, set it upright on a stone and proceeded to turn the handle. To prevent it from jumping around she motioned for one of the braves to hold it in place and continued to grind.

Soon a feeble trickle of cornmeal appeared, causing grunts of surprise and satisfaction from her audience. The new owner of the handmill then went off with his prize to show his wife how to work it, while Mary returned to her stump and pestle chuckling to herself. She knew she could grind more and better cornmeal with those primitive tools than the Indian woman was going to produce with her fancy handmill.

Johnny did not come to sleep with Mary that night – nor ever again.

Chapter 6

BUCKSKIN AND BEAR OIL

Little Doe and Mary were constant companions. Whether they pounded corn in the sunshine before their house or wandered far into the forest in search of fuel for the family fire, they were always together, and from the gentle Indian girl, bit by bit Mary learned to speak the Delaware language.

She discovered that the old couple were known as Red Hawke and Mother Medicine and that Long Arrow was not, as she had supposed, their son but their son-in-law, married to their daughter Bright Star. This couple had three children – a girl of about eight named Humming Bird, a little boy called Chipmunk and a toddler known simply as Baby. The second daughter, Turtledove, was Little Doe's mother, a widow whose husband had been killed in battle.

"That is why the council allowed us to adopt you," explained Little Doe, "to fill his place."

"How can I fill his place? I can't go out on the trail and bring home meat for the family."

"No, but you can marry a brave who will then belong to our family. He will bring in the meat and you will bring us cuddly babies."

Mary kept silent. She realized that her dreams were of white babies – not brown ones.

"White Boy," added Little Doe referring to Johnny, "takes the place of a young brother of the chief who was drowned last year."

Mary saw little of Johnny. He seemed to be possessed by a desire to imitate the boys in Bear Claw's family. On the few occasions when she managed to corner him he was impatient to leave her and join them in their games of skill. He was learning Delaware even faster than she, absorbing it like a sponge.

It worried her that her brother did not appear to grieve for their parents as she did, sobbing to herself in the long lonely nights, and often even in the daytime being obliged to turn her back on people to hide her tears.

One day, however, when Johnny came to see her, he happened to notice the patchwork quilt where it hung inside the buckskin doorflap. "Das ist mein mutter's quilt," he said in the quaint mixture of German and English that he often used, and his lower lip quivered.

"I know, darling. They took it when they – when they captured us." She reached out to draw him to her but he pulled away, biting his lip to steady it.

"Bear Claw says a brave does not cry," he muttered and walked staunchly away.

It was a relief to Mary to know he did remember and care, and she understood now that his violent interest in imitating the braves was his outlet for a grief that was too big for the little fellow to endure. Sometimes she wondered if his way was not better than hers. She was making a point of remembering because deep in her heart was always the hope of being rescued.

Fearing that she might lose all track of time as the days slipped into weeks, she made herself a stick calendar like the one her brother Jake used to have and hung it up inside her bunk.

Gradually she became used to the ways of her new family. They were kind to her and left her free to do as she pleased, but some of their customs seemed strange. There were no set times for meals. Everyone ate when he felt like it – from the pot or supplies beside the fire. The food was good and plentiful, cooked twice a day by the women and similar to what she was accustomed to at home; meat stews, bean soup, hominy cakes, varied with dried pumpkin and berries and, in season, wild onions and spring salad greens.

The men kept the household supplied with meat. Every few days Red Hawke or Long Arrow laid the carcass of some animal across the threshold, a buck or a bear or some smaller creature. The women skinned and butchered it, and then immediately began the process of tanning the hide on a skin frame outside.

Having been trained by her own mother to be a very particular housekeeper Mary insisted on washing her bowl and keeping it hidden in her bunk between meals, much to the amusement of the others who left theirs on the ground and cheerfully shared them with the dogs.

Mary never liked to be untidy. Soon after she arrived she borrowed a bone comb from Little Doe and with it succeeded in removing the tangles from her hair so that she could again plait it neatly in long tawny coloured braids. Every morning she tipped some of the drinking water out of its bark container and washed her hands and face and when possible she bathed in the icy water.

Her homespun dress, however, was filthy and ragged for she had worn it night and day for many weeks.

It had been made of blue linsey-woolsey by her mother years ago in New Jersey when Sarah was only twelve, and had been treasured and worn ever since by each of the Whitmore girls in turn. When wearing it Mary felt close to all of them and that made her fiercely possessive of it. Time and again Mother Medicine urged her to accept a buckskin dress in its stead but each time she refused. She made up her mind to wash the dress in the river as soon as the weather was warm enough.

Two things that Mary found particularly hard to endure were the overpowering odour of bear grease which sometimes became rancid in the hot wigwam, and the incessant itch of insect bites. Each morning when she crawled out of bed scratching and wriggling in distress Mother Medicine offered her the bowl of bear oil, indicating that she should coat herself with it the way the rest of them did. Each time she turned away in disgust from the hated smell and avoided it by escaping out of doors.

One night the insects were so vicious that Mary exhausted by the constant misery whispered, "God please help me. I can't stand this." Next morning, as she sat on the edge of her bunk and watched Bright Star rub Baby's smooth brown skin with the bear oil, the thought suddenly struck her – why does no one scratch but me? Could it be that the bear oil keeps off the insects?

She reached for the bowl and Bright Star, laughing with delight, gave it to her. The relief was instantaneous and unbelievable, as she covered herself from head to toe. Both her problems vanished – the insects now left her alone and, being immersed in the hated odour, she soon became so used to it that she forgot it altogether.

When the weather was warmer, Mary borrowed a tattered old skin dress of Little Doe's to wear and went down where the yellowing willows hung over the river to wash her dress. She found a quiet backwater pool near a low bank and with determination plunged the dress into the water and began to scrub.

At once she saw her mistake. The water was still icy cold and the dress being half wool began at once to shrink. The more she scrubbed the stiffer and smaller it became. Cheering herself with the hope that she might be able to stretch it later she continued to scrub. When she finally hung it up on a branch to dry she found that stretching was out of the question. She was forced to admit that it was now only big enough for an eight-year-old.

She sat down on a log and wept.

Mother Medicine came and sat quietly beside her.

"It is too small. I will have to give it to Humming Bird", sniffed Mary.

The old woman nodded. Then gently from behind her back she produced a brand new doeskin dress fringed around the bottom and over the shoulders and decorated all the way around with coloured embroidery.

"I make this for you, my daughter," said Mother Medicine in Delaware.

Mary was stunned and caught between two conflicting emotions: her desire to cling to her past in the form of the now useless homespun, and the urge to show gratitude to Mother Medicine for her kindness. For a second she struggled within herself, then she threw her arms around the old woman and hugged her. The shy, pleased expression on Mother Medicine's face was her reward.

"Now you real Indian girl."

Mary cringed. That was exactly what she had not wanted to be. With all of her stubborn nature she had been clinging to her white heritage and struggling to pre-serve intact her memories of home. However, she had enough common sense to know when she was beaten. If she was going to live with the Indians she might as well live like the Indians. She slipped out of Little Doe's tat-tered old garment and into the gay new doeskin, turning herself around to show how nice it looked.

Mother Medicine clapped her hands in glee and laughed like a child.

A new relationship was born between them at that moment, a mother-daughter relationship – not that Mary ever forgot her own mother but rather that she grew fond of her Indian one. She learned to appreciate her so much that, to the end of her days when she died at the great age of ninety-one, she liked to tell anyone who would listen to her, "I loved my Indian mother. She was very good to me."

Chapter 7

SPRING ON THE ALLEGHENY

Spring came with swift beauty on the Allegheny and the two girls enjoyed to the full their excursions into the now greening forest. Tree tops were changing from a copper-coloured haze of flowerlets to the tender green of opening leaves. Song birds, back from the south were darting in and out of the bushes in a frenzy of excitement, while underfoot all manner of small creatures were stirring with new life.

Little Doe trained Mary carefully to obey her slightest signal. She always walked ahead and, at a given sign from her, both of them froze motionless until Mary saw whatever it was of beauty or peril that the Indian girl had already spotted: a motionless rabbit watching them, a partridge on its nest in the bracken or, on occasion, danger to be avoided — a deadly copperhead on the trail or a wildcat above them crouched to spring.

When their errand took them far from camp they left a marked trail behind for the return journey. There was no need to hurry because no one cared how much wood they brought home or how long it took them to get it. They were free as the air they breathed.

On the way out they explored, searching for the first pure white blooms of the bloodroot or something to nibble as they went — tasty wild ginger roots or tender coiled fronds of the ferns. On the return journey they attended to business, for their backs were then loaded with heavy bundles of fuel held in place by hempen straps and a tump line around their foreheads. Halfway home they lowered these to the ground for a while and, lying on their backs on a carpet of last year's leaves, gazed up at the blue sky through a tracery of shining buds. Mary loved these times when she seemed to float on a cloud of contentment, forgetting for the moment the agony of the past and the uncertainty of the future. Sometimes they lay on their stomachs on the river bank gazing at reflections in a quiet pool in which the white blossoms of the shadbushes and the dark red masses of dogwood and alder branches were turned upside down in the water.

One day as they set forth they smelled smoke and heard a booming crash in the forest ahead of them.

"That is my friend Fleet Foot," said Little Doe, "He is cutting up a tree for the Spring Planting Ceremony."

Soon they came out into a clearing where a handsome Delaware boy slightly older than they had just felled a tree by burning it through at the base, and was now setting small fires at intervals along the length of the fallen trunk.

"What are those for?" asked Mary of him, pointing to the small fires and putting to use her newly learned Delaware words. The boy ignored her and turning to Little Doe said something in his own tongue that sounded like pennauwonkpitschen.

Little Doe doubled up with laughter.

"What did he say?" Mary asked.

Little Doe shook her head as they moved on. She refused to translate but she did explain that the boy was cutting the tree into short logs by means of the small fires.

"But why burn it? White people would use an axe."

"Tomahawk for killing – keep sharp. Delaware people cut trees with fire before white people came over the sea."

It sounded to Mary like a good idea but she was nettled by the way the boy had ignored her and she made up her mind to find out what he had said that was so funny.

When they were back in the village she approached a group of men playing dice with coloured plum stones and asked them, "What does pennauwonk-pitschen mean?"

To her chagrin they too burst into laughter and shook their heads. She backed away and went to Mother Medicine with the question. The older woman gave her the answer in simpler Delaware words, "White girl asks too many silly questions." No wonder Little Doe and the men had laughed! Mary was furious with that Fleet Foot boy for poking fun at her.

In the days that followed the girls were often surprised by Fleet Foot and a friend of his called the Otter who would ambush them on their way for wood, appearing unexpectedly from nowhere to tease them or chase them or to help them at whatever they were picking at the moment.

One sunny day they took Humming Bird, Chipmunk and Johnny with them for a picnic treat. The Indian children had been thoroughly trained in the importance of obeying the rules of the forest and Little Doe and Mary both tried to explain these to Johnny, hoping he understood. They proceeded in single file, Little Doe in the lead and Johnny bringing up the rear.

When they reached a sunny exposed slope where dainty spring beauties carpeted the ground with their pink and white striped flowers, Little Doe called a halt.

"These are what we call the small forest potatoes," she explained. "In good times Delaware people eat big potatoes or wapatoo but when they are starving they are glad to eat these small potatoes. Look – I show you." She prodded the earth under the flowers with a pointed stick and dug up several of the tiny tubers. Then she made a hole in the ground beside a running creek and built a small fire in it. When the coals were hot enough she roasted the tiny vegetables in them and they sat around the fire and ate them. The little vegetables were not much bigger than a good sized pea, and Mary thought what a lot of digging it would take to collect enough to feed a hungry man.

As they were walking through the bush on their way home Little Doe suddenly gave the signal to freeze. They all stopped dead in their tracks except Johnny, who was in one of his headstrong moods and dashed forward past them all.

Then everything seemed to happen at once. Afterwards Mary could not remember what she noticed first. There was the deadly sound of a rattlesnake on the trail ahead, its coiled yellow body covered with black spots and its venomous forked tongue slithering in and out between poisonous fangs. There was the sudden descent of a large copper coloured body across their path and then a tangle of legs and arms in the bracken to their right where Johnny lay with Fleet Foot on top of him.

Little Doe and the other children began slowly backing away from the snake while Mary ran to Johnny in terror.

"Did it bite you?"

"No."

Mary was so upset by her fears and Johnny's narrow escape that she hardly knew what she was doing. She shook him and scolded him, "You are a naughty boy to disobey. You might have died in a few hours if Fleet Foot had not saved you."

Johnny tossed his head defiantly.

Fleet Foot hushed her. He knelt down beside the little boy and looked him straight in the eye. "In the forest," he said, "no brave ever ignores the sign to freeze."

Johnny hung his head in shame.

The rattler was still there on the path, still rattling the bones in its tail and flicking its vicious forked tongue.

"Kill that thing," ordered Mary, stamping her foot.

"No," said the Otter appearing like magic from behind a bush. "My brother the snake was good. He warned you. If rattlesnake does not warn then Indian kills it".

When they got home Mary consulted Mother Medicine about the rattler. "Would Johnny really have died if it had bitten him?"

"No, my daughter, because he was not alone. Little Doe knew what to do to save him: every Indian does or otherwise they would never be safe when alone in the forest. Come with me now and I will show you what to use to counteract the poison."

After that scare the girls left the children at home when they went to the forest. For a long time they saw no more of Fleet Foot and his friend, for it was not customary for Indian boys to take any notice of girls until they were grown men. Then unexpectedly one day the two boys appeared from behind a fallen log. Fleet Foot, obviously showing off, proceeded to climb the highest tree in sight. There was a crow's nest near the top and it became apparent that his aim was to reach that.

They held their breath as he crawled slowly out on a swaying limb far above the ground and grabbed the nest. His descent was even more daring for he had now only one free hand. He landed safely however, and presented the nest to Little Doe who blushed with pleasure. In the rough mass of twigs and grasses were four eggs splashed with blotches and speckles of grayish green.

The girls built a fire beside a creek and cooked the eggs on hot stones, then the four of them sat around and ate them with handfuls of fresh watercress, and listened to the music of water running over stones. Whenever Fleet Foot glanced at Little Doe she blushed, but when he looked at Mary she turned her head away because she had not yet forgiven him for making fun of her.

Chapter 8

MEDICINE MAID

Johnny came for his sister. "Polly," he said, "Bear Claw has a sore eye and he wants you to doctor it."

"Oh no, I can't do that. Doctoring is Mother Medicine's business."

"She is there already, has been for ages, and she can't do anything to help him. I told him how you used to take grit out of our eyes at home and he said to get you."

"Very well then." Mary got up reluctantly because she feared Mother Medicine's reaction if she should succeed where the old woman failed. She and Johnny walked slowly over to the big wigwam which served as the chief's home and also as the Council House. There they found Bear Claw seated by the fire, his eye inflamed and swollen. Beside him sat Mother Medicine with her pouch full of cures. Mary turned first to her.

"Do you want me to try?"

The old woman nodded.

Mary asked Bear Claw to move into the sunlight at the doorway, then she grasped his eyelid by the lashes and, telling him to look down, she held the lid up. With her keen young sight she was able to see a tiny black speck in the centre of the inflamed area.

"Wait," she said and went to get a smooth twig and a scrap of soft doeskin dipped in oil. She again grasped the chief's eyelid, rolled it up over the little stick, held it there firmly with her left hand while, with one deft sweep of her right, she brushed the oiled doeskin sideways across the sore place and stepped back. The cinder was now plainly visible on the doeskin.

Mary turned to Mother Medicine. "Have you some soothing salve for him?" she asked in a quiet voice. Then she left her to apply this and returned to her skin frame. Soon Mother Medicine joined her there and they worked in silence side by side for some time. After a while Bear Claw came and stood beside them.

"My eye is better now thanks to you, Mother Medicine, and to your daughter, Medicine Maid. You have trained her well."

Mary looked up and opened her mouth to say, "She never taught me that: my own white mother did." She stopped herself just in time, however, remembering that Bear Claw was famous as a chief for his diplomacy. No doubt he was wise to include the old woman in his praise. She lowered her eyes and continued to scrape the pelt.

"Come, Medicine Maid," said Mother Medicine after Bear Claw had moved away. "Now you have earned a new name and we will go together to examine my stores of herbs and see what more we need for doctoring the sick."

Rather than being jealous of Mary's success Mother Medicine was generously offering to share her secrets. "There are many charms and chants that you must learn," she continued, "and I will teach you all the cures that my mother taught me." Together they examined the bunches of dried roots and herbs that Mother

Medicine kept hanging above her bed, and then they went out into the forest in search of growing specimens to compare with them.

When they found a clump of boneset growing in an open, swampy place the old woman began to talk. "It is not always the herb that cures the sick one. Sometimes that fails. What cures him is the will of Manitou and you must know how to ask the Great Spirit to do this. There are two kinds of medicine men – good ones and bad. Good medicine men are humble and seek the help of Manitou, then they let him work the cure. Bad medicine men pretend they know everything. They fool the patient with signs and wonders or frighten him with false faces and other tricks."

Mary nodded her understanding. She remembered vividly the night her mother and she had applied the onion cure to the baby's croup without results until they had prayed for help.

"Here's how you do it." Mother Medicine produced a small amount of Indian tobacco from her pouch and digging a little hole to the east of the boneset plant she placed the tobacco in the hole and covered it over, lighting up her own pipe at the same time and saying, "Grandfather, here is a smoke offering of tobacco. I earnestly pray that you will take pity on the sick one. I wish for him to get well forever of that which is causing pain in his body. For with you alone rests the spiritual power sufficient to bless anyone. – I am thankful Grandfather, also Creator, that you grant our appeal this day for all we ask."

"Now," she said. "We leave this first boneset plant to grow and find a second healthy one which we will gather for our medicine. We will take it home and dry it in the sun. We must perform this rite," she continued, "before gathering a plant for medicinal use because the Great Creator has given a spiritual nature to each plant as sensitive as our own spirits."

Mary had always wanted to heal the sick and here, she felt, was her chance to learn how to do it. She longed for a special occupation of some kind to fill her time and thoughts. Johnny was training himself to become a Delaware warrior and she was now going to train herself to become a Delaware shaman.

It was a busy time of year. Once *Wekolis* the whip-poorwill, was heard to give his plaintive cry and the leaf of the white oak was as big as a mouse's ear, the women said to each other, "It is time to go planting corn." So as soon as the spring planting ceremony was over the men and older boys set out on the deer hunt, while the women and girls went to work in the fields.

This was a much pleasanter occupation than Mary had anticipated. An older woman organized the work so it was evenly divided and they all kept together in order to talk and joke with each other while they planted the corn in little hillocks with pumpkin, bean, pea and melon seeds sown around them. Through the summer months they tended the fields, hoeing between the hillocks, and the corn grew tall and beautiful above their heads.

They worked at an easy pace with plenty of rests in the shade. During the hot weather Mary and Little Doe swam in the river in their rest periods with few or no clothes on, splashing each other and whatever children they were caring for at the moment. Late in August, or as the Delawares said, "in the moon when the corn is in the milk," all this freedom came to an abrupt end.

A troop of horsemen rode in over the hills one day, shooting off their guns and riding right down into the village as if they belonged there. Mary watched with a sort of horrified fascination as the foremost warrior rode around the village displaying a red pole to which were attached eight dressed scalps. The smallest of these gruesome trophies had yellow hair. The scene brought back to her the grief and terror of the massacre of her own family. "Who are they?" she whispered to Little Doe through stiff lips.

"They are the Weasel and his braves returning from the warpath. Word came to us sometime ago that they had been defeated in two battles and had lost five of our men. A few scalps they bring but no captives. No wonder they sneak home when Bear Claw and the other braves are not here to scoff at them."

"Which one is the Weasel?"

"That sly looking man with the jagged scar on his cheek. Nobody likes him. He wanted to be chief but people didn't trust him so they elected Bear Claw instead and the Weasel has been jealous of Bear Claw ever since."

Some of the Weasel's men were seriously wounded and Mother Medicine said to Mary, "Come, we will be needed. Collect as much spagnum moss and slippery elm as you can carry and meet me at our place." When Mary returned with her arms full she found her Indian mother mixing a potent *beson* or cure in boiling water over the fire, carefully stirring from left to right. As soon as this was ready she took Mary with her to the wigwam of the wounded men.

Treating her like an apprentice, Mother Medicine gave her jobs to do such as holding a bowl of ointment or bathing the patient's brow, all the time explaining to her the exact treatment that was needed and which herbs to use. They attended to the most serious case first, a young brave who had been unconscious when they carried him in, flushed with a high fever from a festering bullet wound in his upper arm.

The smell of the yellow pus from the wound was so nauseating that it almost made Mary vomit. However, she firmly bit her lip and held the bowl while Mother Medicine cleaned out the wound, disinfected it with a preparation of white oak bark, removed the buried bullet with a sharp knife, and then treated the wound with a decoction of lichen and slippery elm. Finally she dressed the whole with spagnum moss to absorb the blood, and applied a poultice of white walnut bark to relieve pain and hasten the healing process.

"Now," said Mother Medicine, "we will give him boneset for his fever. We will keep the wound open for several weeks until it cleanses itself and then it will be safe to let it close and heal."

Although he was conscious now, not a sign of suffering showed on the patient's face throughout all this treatment. He lay there totally controlled, much to Mary's admiration.

The work force in the fields had become sadly depleted, since Mother Medicine and Mary were busy with the wounded warriors and the wives of the returned braves were needed at home to cook and care for them. One September evening Mary worked late by the light of the harvest moon, trying to make up her share of the hoeing. Suddenly she felt uncomfortable, as though someone were near her although she had not heard a sound. She looked up to find the man with the scarred face standing watching her. He began to walk slowly around her. "And who might you be?" he said in a sneering tone.

"I am Mother Medicine's adopted daughter," answered Mary in a loud voice hoping someone might be near enough to hear and come to her rescue.

Mother Medicine appeared like magic from behind the tall cornstalks. "What do you want, my brother?"

"Nothing. I was just admiring your daughter." And the man sauntered off.

"He frightened me," whispered Mary.

"I know. Keep away from him. He is a bad Indian. He has already had two wives and they both left him with the full consent of the Council Ring. I hope he is not looking for another." Mary hoped so too. She made a point after that of never working in the fields alone.

Between the harvesting of the crops and the return of the deer hunters, Mary found a little spare time in which to have a private talk with Johnny. It was in the harvest moon, when the leaves of the forest were scarlet and gold and the bluejays called raucously to each other, that she led him to a secret place on a willow branch sloping out above the river. Here they were hidden from sight by the foliage. Seated side by side they swung their legs and listened to the plunk, plunk of the fish in the river or gazed at the distorted reflections of their own faces in the quiet pool below them.

"Johnny, I discovered from Long Arrow that Jake and the girls in the Sugar Bush were not found. They must still be alive and some day I am sure Jake will come to rescue us, or he will send someone else for us and we must be ready when that happens. We must be able to tell them who we are and where we came from, so we should practice now before we forget how to speak in English. I'll pretend that I am a British soldier who rides into camp some day and questions you like this:

"Hello, little boy, what is your name?"

"My name is Johnny Whitmore," he answered.

"And how old are you?"

"I am four years old."

"Who was your father?"

"Peter Whitmore."

"And where did he live?"

"He lived in – I don't know. Polly, I don't want to do this. I want to go and shoot squirrels with my new bow and arrow."

"No, Johnny, not yet. Answer the question first. Learn the answers and then you can go. Sarah told me to do this. Say: 'My father was killed near Shamokin in Pennsylvania on Easter Sunday in 1780.' Say it Johnny."

He struggled to oblige her and she was shocked to see how much he had already forgotten. "Once a year in bluejay time I am going to ask you those questions, so you will remember the answers. Now, say it all over again, then you can go and shoot with your new bow."

Sarah was right, she thought as he scampered off. He is forgetting his English.

When the men were home from the chase the great Harvest Festival was held and for the first time Mary felt like taking part in the festivities. She had helped to grow the corn, the people were no longer strangers to her, and she had become accustomed enough to the wild war whoops of the braves that they no longer terrified her.

It was with some excitement, therefore, that she joined Bright Star, Turtledove and Little Doe in their preparations for the big feast and dance. She helped them bake the special bread made from corn-in-the-milk and to roast the venison brought home by the hunters. When all the cooking was done, they arrayed themselves in their best for the dance with much giggling. One round red spot on each cheek was all the paint thought proper and modest for an Indian maiden. They slicked their hair with bear oil until it shone in the firelight, and wore their best doeskin dresses and beaded moccasins for the occasion. Some of the women in the wigwams of the Weasel's men were decking themselves out in red cotton skirts and white overblouses, part of the loot brought home by their warriors from a wrecked trading post; but the women of Mother Medicine's family preferred the traditional Delaware dresses of doeskin with fringed borders around the shoulders and below the knees and leggings to match.

In the dances the men in full war paint went first leaping, stamping and yelling. The women followed them, moving quietly and gracefully. Mary danced between Bright Star and Little Doe, trying to match her steps to theirs and to catch the rhythm of the drum: a long stride forward, a short one back so they progressed slowly without seeming effort like smoothly flowing water.

Between dances various warriors recited the stories of their bravest deeds and women sang plaintive songs. Mary found her knowledge of Delaware still inadequate to catch the full meaning of these songs but she enjoyed the lilting music and the sweet voices of the women.

Then Turtledove stood up to sing. Mary caught a word or two here and there, it seemed to her to be a lament for her dead husband and a summary of all his virtues. Mary let it flow in one ear and out the other without paying too much attention until she heard her own name mentioned and felt a nudge in the ribs from Little Doe. This made her sit up and listen carefully. Towards the end of her song Turtledove repeated the theme like a refrain and this time Mary caught the gist of it:

"Our brave warrior
   has gone to the happy hunting grounds
but now has come to us
   a sister to fill his moccasins
and ease the pain of his departure,
   an adopted sister
whose blood now runs red instead of white
   whose laughter ripples in the moonlight
and whose healing hand has earned for her
   the fine new name of Medicine Maid."

Chapter 9

TRIAL BY FIRE

Mary and Johnny settled into the rhythm of their new life and the months and years slipped slowly by. They were busy and, in a way, contented. Every autumn in bluejay time Mary put Johnny through his paces. Pretending to be a British officer, she would question him: "How old are you little boy?"

And year by year the answer changed: "I am five – six – seven – eight."

They had lived for four years with the Delaware when Johnny went through his trial by fire. Mary had no idea beforehand what was going to happen. She only knew that he was looking forward to some special secret ceremony.

"I am going to prove that I am brave enough to become a real Delaware warrior," he boasted.

That was all Mary knew until the dreadful day when she smelled the burning flesh. She and Little Doe were curing beaver pelts behind their wigwam when they noticed the men gathering in the Council House. With them were six little boys, Johnny among them. Two of the children were Bear Claw's sons. All of them were older than Johnny.

Mary felt uneasy but she kept assuring herself that

all must be well since the chief's own sons were included in the proceedings. Then she noticed the smell and just as it began to dawn on her what it was she heard a piercing scream.

For one second she stood paralyzed. Then she hurled herself across the intervening space and into the Council House. It was only ten seconds later that she was forcibly lifted into the air and removed from the big wigwam, but in that short time she knew what the smell was and the cause of it.

Five boys stood around the central fire, their arms outstretched, palms upward and on the tender inner flesh of those arms were rows of red hot burning coals. Johnny was one of the five. The sixth boy, writhing in agony on the ground, was Bear Claw's youngest son.

That much she saw before Long Arrow swept her off her feet and, in a grip of iron, carried her protesting across the campsite. He literally threw her on the ground at Mother Medicine's feet and, in a tone of deep anger such as she had never heard from him before, said, "Keep her."

Mother Medicine put her arms around the sobbing girl and led her away into the forest. "Hurry", she said. "We must gather balm poplar buds and make healing salve for their arms. Quickly, quickly, help me to pick them." Actually this was a ruse to get Mary away and keep her occupied, for the old woman knew she had plenty of the salve previously prepared and ready for use. By the time they returned to the village the cruel ceremony was over. One of the men beckoned them to come and, armed with bowls of the soothing lotion, the two of them hastened to the Council House.

The five boys were still standing with their arms extended and their faces set to hide any sign of suffering.

At the soothing touch of the salve there was a little gasp of relief from Johnny and through gritted teeth he muttered, "I did it, Polly."

"Yes, you are very brave. I'm proud of you." She had a hard time to keep from crying.

The five young heroes were led to a cool shady spot where they could sit and receive the congratulations of the whole village. One after another the adult braves walked past the boys to do them honour – five potential Delaware warriors headed for fame in the forest and on the warpath. The sixth boy was utterly broken up at his own failure in the trial of courage.

When it was all over Mary went behind her own wigwam and was sick. Not since the massacre four years before had she felt such agony of soul.

Wisely, Mother Medicine kept her very busy for the next while searching for rare herbs, drying them and then pounding them into powders to be mixed together in various medicinal concoctions. It was miraculous how quickly Johnny's arms healed: the salve had been a potent one. But he bore the scars of this trial by fire to the end of his days.

A month or so later Mother Medicine decided to take Mary and Little Doe with her on a two-week expedition in search of herbs. Certain rare plants were hard to find in quantities large enough for her medicinal needs, and she felt that the two girls could learn much on the excursion.

The three of them set forth in fine fettle, taking with them very little except a blanket each to sleep in and baskets in which to bring home their trophies. Some jerked venison and sweetened cornmeal were all the provisions needed as they expected to fish and to snare small animals on the way.

The first day out they walked a long distance and made camp on the banks of a strange stream. Having no household duties they could give all their attention to the study of wild plants. They took heed where they grew, how they looked in their native haunts, how they smelled and felt, and particularly how they compared with other plants of a similar appearance but of deadly content. The old woman drilled the girls endlessly in recognizing the poisonous specimens that were to be avoided.

Mary was fascinated and worked hard. If she were going to be a doctor she wanted to be a good one. Little Doe, on the other hand, was not very interested. She took life easy, preferring to swim in the river while the others worked, or to lie on her back gazing at the sky.

"I think I like babies best," she said, "not medicine – lots of cuddly babies."

"You'd better not have more than two or three then," advised her grandmother, "or there will come a year of famine and you won't be able to feed them all. Now, without moving from where you are show me something you could eat if you were starving."

Little Doe sat up and pointed to a group of arrowhead shaped leaves held above the water on stiff stems. "There," she said, "Indian potatoes or *wapatoo*."

"Yes, dig some up and show Medicine Maid how to prepare them."

Little Doe plunged into the stream and with her bare toes pulled up any number of tuberous roots, cleaned them and roasted them in the coals of their campfire. They were somewhat like the potatoes Mary remembered back home in Pennsylvania, but smaller and narrower in shape and they had a different taste.

"These," said Little Doe," are a different kind of potato from the little forest ones we used to find with Fleet Foot and the Otter."

Later as they were slowly working their way upstream under overhanging branches, Little Doe gave the sign to freeze. Mary stood motionless, hardly breathing as she glanced from side to side to see where the danger lay. But there was no danger this time. It was beauty that Little Doe had stopped to admire.

Across the river was an almost perfect circle of blue-black shadow surrounded by overhanging light-green foliage, and standing straight and startlingly beautiful in the centre against the dark background was a clump of vivid red flowers. The whole scene was reflected in a still pool of water below it.

"The cardinal flowers that we came for," exclaimed Mother Medicine. "The root of this plant is a cure for the white man's terrible fever – the one they call 'typhoid'."

They went home at the end of the two weeks very proud of themselves, their baskets full of rare roots and unusual herbs. Red Hawke and Bright Star greeted them rather soberly in their own house. Mary immediately set out to find Johnny and tell him she was back.

She could not find him anywhere. Before long she began to realize something was wrong. There was a strangeness in the manner of each person she asked; they either replied that they had not seen him or turned their backs to her in silence. The more she searched the more alarmed she became. What could be wrong? Where could Johnny be?

Mother Medicine met her with open arms at the doorflap when she returned. "My daughter," she said gently, pressing Mary's face against her bosom "My daughter, they tell me White Boy has gone."

"Gone!" gasped Mary, terrified. "Do you mean he is dead?"

"No. Gone. A British officer came on horseback and carried him away to Canada."

Beaded purse given to John Whitmore by his adopted Indian mother. Now in the Fort George Museum at Niagara-on-the-Lake, Ontario.

Chapter 10

FLEET FOOT

Mary was wild with anguish, her pain a mixture of personal disappointment and loneliness. Johnny had gone to their own white people and she was left by herself in the Indian village.

Perhaps it was not yet too late to follow his trail? She went to ask the Chief.

"No – too late. They have been gone ten days. I too grieve for White Boy," said Bear Claw. "If I had been here it would never have happened. The Weasel let him go because he was jealous of me having such a fine adopted brother."

"Can't you find out where the man was taking him and why he didn't take me too?"

"You were not here, my daughter, and White Boy speaks no English now to tell about his white sister."

This was true. She had forgotten that all the English which Johnny now knew was the memory-work she had taught him, and in that there was no mention of a sister.

"But the Weasel knew he had a sister. Why didn't he tell the British officer about me?" Even as she asked the question she knew the answer – the Weasel had reasons of his own for wanting her to stay. "Won't you please ask the Weasel the man's name and where he came from?"

"You may ask him yourself but how are you to know if the answer he gives you is the truth?"

Sadly Mary gave up for she knew the Weasel's reputation for doubletalk. Overcome with dull despair she left the Council House and, like a wounded animal, sought solitude in her pain. She went away by herself to her secret place in the willow that hung over the water, the place where she and Johnny had so often practised their English. Oh, why had she ever made up that story about a British officer riding into camp to take Johnny away? When a real British officer had come her brother had, apparently, remembered the story and gone without protest.

And why was she so miserable? Shouldn't she be glad for Johnny's sake that he was again with white people and would never be a Delaware warrior expected to scalp and torture his prisoners? Yes, she was glad for him but for herself she was desolate.

She was reasoning this way, idly swinging her legs and gazing down at the distorted reflections beneath her when she noticed something that made her heart stand still – there were two faces, not one, reflected in the pool!

With a tremendous effort she forced herself to turn and see who had come silently to sit beside her on the willow branch. She found herself looking deep into a pair of shining dark eyes filled with kindness.

"I too miss White Boy", said Fleet Foot.

Mary sensed in his gaze not only sympathy but something more – a personal interest in her that flustered her yet somehow eased her grief. They sat there in silence for a while watching the fish jump and then Mary indicated that she must go home.

As she entered the wigwam Little Doe passed her without speaking. This struck her as unusual but she was too absorbed in her grief to probe for the reason. When Little Doe came home again she turned her back without speaking and Mary felt very uncomfortable. What could be wrong?

Next morning Mary worked hard pounding corn and then wandered down to the river and headed for the willow tree. At the edge of her consciousness hovered a thought, a sort of warning against going there. Whatever the thought was she did not pause to find out. She pushed it aside and climbing out on the willow branch, sat dangling her legs over the water.

After a while she saw a second face reflected in the pool and knew that Fleet Foot had come again to keep her company. He held out his hand, palm upward. On it lay a lovely blue robin's egg.

Mary felt her face grow hot as she thanked and accepted the gift. Clearly in her mind's eye rose the picture of a blushing Little Doe accepting crow's eggs from this same boy four springs before in the forest. Always Fleet Foot had been Little Doe's special friend so what was she doing sitting here with him on the willow branch? She felt confused, although comforted by his attention. They sat companionably there for a while and then she left to attend to some of her patients on the far side of the village.

When Mary reached home she found Fleet Foot's mother visiting with Mother Medicine in the doorway of their lodge, both women laughing and talking. Beside them lay the carcass of a deer. Mary smiled politely to excuse herself as she pushed past them into the wigwam to get a tool she needed for scraping skins. Inside she came face to face with Little Doe, and to her horror she saw in her friend's eyes unmistakable hate.

She felt as if someone had poured a bucket of ice cold water over her. Too stunned and hurt to think clearly, she grabbed the scraping tool and stumbled outside. A numbness settled over her heart and mind. Life was too difficult to understand: Johnny had gone; her best friend had turned against her; and, in the pit of her stomach, was a horrible lump caused by the suspicion that she herself might somehow be to blame for this last trouble – that she could find an explanation if she were brave enough to be honest with herself.

She worked feverishly at the beaver pelt to keep from thinking, from wondering where Johnny was now, from regretting that she had been out of camp when the man came for him, from facing whatever it was that had caused Little Doe to hate her.

Mother Medicine joined her. "Fleet Foot's mother came to visit me," she said. "She brought the gift of a deer from him and the request for you to marry her son."

So that was it! The thing she had sensed but had refused to face, the something more than sympathy that she had seen in Fleet Foot's eyes and which had made her hot and confused. Now she knew why Little Doe hated her, and that it had been a mistake to encourage him by going back to the willow branch the second time.

Mother Medicine was still standing beside her, waiting. "What is your answer, my daughter. Will you go with Fleet Foot as his wife, or not? If you say 'no' then the deer must be returned at once before it spoils."

Mary dropped the scraping tool and held her burning face in both hands. "Wait," she said, "please wait," and she turned and ran. Where could she go to be private and think? She dared not go again to her secret willow for Fleet Foot would find her there. Just then her eye fell on the empty sweathouse, a little hut used by women with rheumatism when they took the steam bath cure. That would do. She crawled into it on her hands and knees through the low doorway and crouched there in the dark.

At first her mind was blank. Then into it came the memory of her mother's voice saying, "If you are ever in trouble or alone – remember that God loves you. Ask Him for help. Trust Him and an answer will come."

"Dear God," she prayed, "please help me now for I am alone, dreadfully alone and in trouble. Should I marry Fleet Foot? And what can I do about Little Doe?"

Gradually her mind cleared as she realized that to her Fleet Foot was only a friend – a good one, handsome, brave and kind, but only a friend. She did not want to marry him and live with him forever. She saw now that her excitement and confusion had been caused not by love but by being flattered by his attention. Little Doe was the one who really loved him and should marry him.

How well she remembered the look of wonder on Little Doe's face the day she explained Indian marriage customs. "Fleet Foot and I are free to marry," she had said, "because our mothers belong to different clans. His mother is a Turtle and mine belongs to the Wolf clan. There are three clans among the Delaware: the Turtle, the Wolf and the Turkey. We belong to our mothers' clans and must marry someone from a different one. If Fleet Foot and I had both been turtles or both wolves our families would long ago have stopped us from being such special friends."

Mary knew now what she must do. She must go quickly and say "no" to Fleet Foot's proposal. As for Little Doe, she could think of nothing in the world that would heal her hurt pride.

She crawled out through the hole in the sweat-house and went to Mother Medicine. "Please say thank you to Fleet Foot for me. Tell him I admire him very much but I don't want to marry anyone."

Without a word Mother Medicine shouldered the carcass and returned it to Fleet Foot's mother. Nothing more was ever said on the subject. Soon afterwards the men, Fleet Foot among them, left on the spring deer hunt.

Mary and Little Doe worked together in the corn-fields all summer without speaking and Mary was lone-lier than she had ever been before.

Preparations for the great Harvest Ceremony were underway when one day Mary, who was doctoring a woman for a toothache, noticed Fleet Foot's mother again visiting with Mother Medicine.

She went home to find a radiant Little Doe prepar-ing something over the fire. "We have a treat," she said, "Fleet Foot brought me six beaver tails and I have accepted them."

"Oh, I am so glad, so very glad." Mary knew that her friend meant she had accepted Fleet Foot as well as his gift.

"I'm making corn and cranberry pudding fla-voured with hickory nut oil for my return gift," contin-ued Little Doe. "If you like you can help me pound the roasted nuts into powder and boil them to separate the oil."

"I'd love to help," answered Mary and meant it. She meant too that she was glad to be again on speaking terms with her friend and thankful that Little Doe was not too proud to accept Fleet Foot's proposal.

Turtledove delivered her daughter's return gift to the bridegroom's family, while Little Doe dressed carefully in her best doeskins and was ready and waiting when Fleet Foot came to get her. The newly-marrieds then spent the night in a friend's wigwam and next morning began making one for themselves.

Mary was surprised. "I thought they would be part of our family and live here with us," she said to Bright Star, "the way you and Long Arrow did when you were married."

"Yes, they are part of our family," answered Bright Star, "and they will come and live with us some day but young couples often like to have a place of their own for a few moons when they are first married."

For their wedding present the women of the family decided to work together and finish the turkey feather blanket which they had been making the previous winter. They got busy at once twisting and knotting the fine hempen cord so that the feathers lay one on top of another the way they had done on the live birds.

The two boys, Chipmunk and Baby, went out and gathered a skinful of hickory nuts for their gift. Long Arrow decided to give his new hunting knife and Red Hawke produced a valuable string of wampum for his present.

Mary's fingers shook in her effort to hurry. Through the open doorflap she could see people gathering: men, women and children forming into a procession with their presents of food, tobacco and cooking pots. Little Doe and Fleet Foot were already seated at the threshold of their new wigwam waiting to receive them.

"Hurry, hurry," urged Humming Bird, "or we will

be late."

"Patience," said her grandmother, "just a few more knots."

When it was finished they stood up to admire their handiwork. "Its lovely," said Mary, "So soft and light. It will make a really warm coverlet."

"We must go now," said Mother Medicine, and together the family joined the procession.

Chapter 11

PLOT AND COUNTERPLOT

The winter following Little Doe's marriage was unusually severe and game was scarce. Gone were the days when Long Arrow might bring home from fifty to a hundred deer in a season. He was lucky now if he shot any at all, and the family was reduced to eating the flesh of animals they had previously scorned to use for food: wildcat, muskrat, fox – even wolf.

The Delawares blamed the poor hunting on expanding white settlements which were destroying the forest and with it their livelihood. They were particularly bitter against the Long Knives, as they called the Americans, who were pouring westward over the Allegheny Mountains by the thousands in search of land. They felt more friendly towards the British who operated out of Canada, attempting, in partnership with some western tribes to stem this settlement in order to preserve the forest and the fur trade.

When the men met in the Council Ring to discuss important matters Mary and the other women made an outer circle around them and listened attentively to all that was said. In this way they gathered information about what was happening in the outside world.

She learned that the Revolutionary War had ended in victory for the Long Knives, so that the British and their sympathizers among the colonists had been obliged to move north into Canada.

She heard also that the border forts of Niagara, Detroit and Michilimackinac were still in British hands, although the treaty that ended the war had given them to the Long Knives. Rumour said this was because the latter had not fulfilled all their treaty obligations.

In her own mind Mary decided that Detroit must be the place to which the British officer had taken Johnny. She had no reason for such a conclusion but it gave her something to think about when she was blue and bored.

Detroit, so the men said, was situated a long way to the west of them in the country of their cousins of the Huron or Wyandotte tribe. Stationed there were Butler's Rangers and other British regiments. They spoke often of a man in Detroit named Colonel McKee who spoke Delaware as well as other Indian languages.

Armed with this knowledge Mary began to daydream about going to Detroit in search of Johnny. Once there she planned to find this Colonel McKee and ask him to help her locate her brother. How she could possibly get there she had no idea but it cheered her to think about it while pounding corn.

One day the Weasel approached. "You work well," he said, trying to flatter her. Mary just nodded without looking up. "I have come to you for help," he added, holding out a cut and bleeding arm.

"I'll get Mother Medicine," said Mary, diving into the wigwam.

"I think he cut it on purpose to get you to doctor him," said Mother Medicine afterwards.

"I know. He is driving me crazy," answered Mary.

"Everywhere I go he is there before me trying to make me speak to him or just staring at me in that nasty way he has."

"My daughter, most Delaware girls are married by the time they have sixteen summers as you have. Indians never force their children to marry but we do give them advice. Why don't you accept some good Delaware youth who will then provide for you and, if necessary, protect you from men like the Weasel?"

Mary sadly shook her head. "I don't want to marry anyone."

In spite of the scarcity of game some of the expert hunters did occasionally kill a buck. When this happened it was instantly cut up and divided among all the families in the village. Therefore Mary was surprised one day, to see the whole carcass of a deer beside their doorflap.

"That," said Mother Medicine, "was brought by the Weasel's sister, Basket Woman. It is for you. He is asking you to marry him."

"No – no never!" said Mary, vehemently.

The old woman just shouldered the deer and returned it to Basket Woman. Before long they could smell the tantalizing aroma of venison cooking in every wigwam but their own. They were desperately hungry for meat, nevertheless they made a joke of it. "I'd rather live with an empty stomach," said Red Hawke, "than live with the Weasel for a son-in-law."

According to Delaware custom that should have been the end of the matter but it was not. The Weasel was a determined man and he now began a campaign aimed to wear down Mary's resistance. He made her miserable by waylaying her at every turn.

Mother Medicine thought up a scheme which she

hoped would put an end to this. "His sister," she said, "has been asking me for a long time to give her a *beson*, a cure for her illness. I have refused because I know her ailment is incurable. If I doctor her and she dies people will say my medicine is no good. But for you, my daughter, I will do it – on condition she makes her brother leave you alone."

This scheme worked well. The Weasel bothered Mary no more as long as his sister lived.

The next summer Little Doe had a baby son whom she named Cricket. Mary adored Cricket. She had been dreadfully lonesome ever since Johnny left, and it was fun and comforting to have a new baby in the family. Little Doe understood this and was generous about sharing her baby.

During the spring and summer moons the food situation eased somewhat as they augmented their slender diet with all kinds of roots, greens and berries and waited for the new crop to ripen. To their horror most of the corn failed to mature that year.

A second severe winter followed this disaster and the situation was grave. It was not only food they lacked; it was ammunition as well. Without good pelts to exchange at the trading posts their credit was running out.

Towards the end of the winter, in the moon when the frogs begin to croak, Basket Woman died and her brother started to pester Mary once more.

The corn crop failed again the second time and Bear Claw, rather than risk a third winter on starvation rations, called his counsellors together to decide on some drastic action. Mary was unable to attend this emergency meeting as she was busy at the time doctoring a child. When she heard the decision they had reached she could hardly believe her ears. They were going to Detroit!

The men had heard from some passing Shawnees that the British at Detroit were giving out free ammunition to friendly tribes. Their plan was to kill and eat the horses and dogs to give them strength for the long journey and be prepared to leave the next morning.

When Mary arose in the morning the Delaware village on the Allegheny, which had been her home for seven years, looked much as it had always done. An hour later not a wigwam was standing. Each family rolled up its bedding skins, packed its remaing food supplies in bags and baskets, collected a few precious cooking pots and carried everything to the canoes. Then they were off.

Down the Allegheny to its junction with the Monegehela, then west on the Ohio to the mouth of the Muskingum, and north on that river to the headwaters of its most westerly tributary lay their route by water. Their plan was to cache their canoes there and proceed on foot to Detroit.

They camped the first night on the banks of the Allegheny several miles above Fort Pitt, which they planned to bypass in the dark having no desire to tangle with the Long Knives there.

Perhaps it was extra strength from the horse flesh she had eaten or the exhilaration of adventure; whatever was the cause, Mary felt happier than she had for a long time as she and Humming Bird brought in wood and began laying their fire. She looked up to find the Weasel standing watching her and all the happiness drained away as fear of him gripped her. At every encampment it was the same thing: the Weasel was always hovering near – a sinister presence, watching and waiting.

Snow was upon them before they arrived at the

upper reaches of the Muskingum and cached the canoes. A long hard trek overland lay ahead. On the trail the women and children were placed in the middle for protection, while the men walked ahead and on both sides. The girls carried the younger children – the women the heavy bundles. The men carried nothing. They had to be armed and prepared for instant action because on them depended the safety of the whole group.

They had proceeded in this fashion for several days when Mary was wakened one night by a sound that, at first, she took to be wolves howling in the distance. Then she realized that the noise was close at hand. It was the plaintive mourning cry of a woman in sorrow and it was coming from Mother Medicine. Red Hawke had left them.

They buried him in a shallow grave in the forest with full warrior honours, his tomahawk and scalping knife at his head and bark vessels of food beside him. Scarce and precious though their provisions were, every member of the family contributed to these supplies to feed his spirit on its long journey to the Happy Hunting Grounds. Then they covered the grave with slabs of bark, and stones to hold them down, picked up their packs and moved on towards Detroit.

Mother Medicine, worn out by grief and hunger, as well as great age, looked exhausted as she struggled along under her heavy load. But she was still alert, for her wisdom was needed. She was their shaman, their wise one, who more than anyone else understood how to find emergency foods beneath the deepening snow. At her direction they broke ice on the creeks and pulled out wapatoo, big Indian potatoes or collected and ate the inner bark of white birch trees. Once they camped near a swamp and she showed the girls how to make flour from the frozen roots of the cattails. Then, suddenly, there was the sound of children's laughter, as the smell of cooking dropcakes was wafted to them through the bare tree trunks.

On and on they went, stumbling from weakness but never complaining, never giving up. South of Sandusky they met a group of Mingoes, or Western Senecas, coming home from Detroit. They had food which they generously shared with the Delawares. They told how the British had given them free ammunition but they were mysteriously silent as to how they had obtained the food supplies.

Farther on they met another group returning from Detroit, Kaskaskis this time and equally secretive about their plentiful provisions. It was Humming Bird who solved the riddle; she became chummy with one of the Kaskaski girls and from her learned that they had sold two captive white boys to the British for the food.

Turtledove was indignant. "No wonder those Mingoes and Kaskaskis kept the source of their food supplies hidden. They were ashamed to admit that they had done such a thing!"

"We Delawares would never sell an adopted captive," added Bright Star.

Mother Medicine was strangely silent. After a while she took Mary aside for a private talk. "My husband," she said, "has gone to the Happy Hunting Grounds and it won't be many moons until I follow him. Then you, my daughter, will have no one to advise you. I have thought of a way to help you escape from the Weasel. Is that what you want?"

"Yes, oh yes," breathed Mary.

"By this scheme you can shoot three crows with one arrow: you will escape forever from the Weasel; you will be able to search for White Boy; and you can help the tribe by providing us with food."

"How can I do all that?"

"By persuading the counsellors to sell you to the British in Detroit for food. Tell them you really want to go and search for White Boy. Once there you will be free from the Weasel, but nothing needs to be said about that because our people know you dislike him and they will understand."

Mary jumped at the chance. "I can't bear to leave you, my mother, but I'd like to search for Johnny and I'd be proud to provide food for our people."

"Good, then let's go and talk to the Chief."

Bear Claw listened gravely when they put the proposition to him. He understood why Mary wanted to go but he was careful to express no opinion. "I will put the matter before my counsellors," he said, and that night he called them together on a high plateau surrounded by pines.

It was cold and dark when Mary and the others gathered around the fire. Her heart beat painfully for everything depended on the decision reached that night. Would the Weasel manage to block the plan? Would the Delaware warriors be willing to set aside their proud traditions and agree to sell a captive – an adopted daughter of the tribe?

The braves smoked in silence for some time then Bear Claw rose and addressed the gathering with great dignity. "Our daughter, Medicine Maid," he said, "who has been a true Delaware for seven summers, wants to leave us and live in Detroit so that she can search for White Boy. She asks us to sell her to the Whites for food. She says it will make her happy to know that her family

93

and friends will again have full stomachs. What is your opinion in this matter?"

Each man then rose in turn and spoke at length without interruption to a rapt audience. As one finished with the words, "I have spoken," and sat down, another rose to give his opinion. The Weasel sat still, expressionless and silent. Long Arrow on behalf of Mary's family spoke of the joy it had been to have her with them and how much they would miss her but he ended by saying they were willing to let her go in search of White Boy since that was her wish.

Bear Claw turned to Mary, "Have you anything to say, my daughter?"

Mary rose, her knees shaking, and with some difficulty found her voice. "I have been happy," she said, "in the wigwams of the Delaware and my heart grieves at the thought of leaving you but I want to go to Detroit to search for White Boy. I love my family and it hurts me to see them starving. If the British will give food in exchange for me then I beg you to let me go."

"What is your wish?" asked Bear Claw turning to the braves. "Shall we let our daughter go in search of White Boy?"

There was silence in the Council Ring except for the sighing of the wind in the pines. Then one by one each man solemnly nodded his head and it was understood that Mary's request had been granted.

For some time past they had seen signs of settlement – burnt stumps and cleared fields even farm homes. Next morning they came out into an open space before the fort, or rather the forts, for there were two of them joined together by a long stockade; Old Fort Pontchartrain on the river to their right and new Fort Lernoult standing square and strong on a rise of ground behind it.

From a bastion fluttered the union flag of Britain and on the walls were redcoated soldiers.

Her father's flag – her father's people! Mary could hardly breathe, the suspense was so great. Was she really going inside those walls? Was she really going to find Johnny?

There was protocol to be observed. Only the most important men of the tribe could enter and treat with the officials in the Council House in the Old Fort. Bear Claw, Long Arrow and two other senior counsellors disappeared through the gate, while Mary and the others waited patiently outside.

Finally the Chief and counsellors returned accompanied by a tall dignified man in a red uniform trimmed with gold lace. With him was a small man, a French Canadian farmer leading a horse and sleigh, the latter piled high with bags and boxes of provisions. He wore a thick natural-coloured blanket coat tied around the waist with a gaily coloured woven sash. On his head was a bright red stocking cap that hung over one side giving him a jaunty air.

The tall man turned out to be Colonel McKee who spoke to them in Delaware asking for the white girl to come forward.

Mary stepped up to him.

"Do you know your own white name?" he asked her.

"Yes. It's Mary Whitmore."

"And do you understand the terms of this bargain – namely that you will be bought by René LeBlanc here for fifty dollars worth of food on condition that you work for him and his wife in their home for twelve moons from today, and then gain your freedom to go wherever you wish? If you agree, I take it you are giving your word as a Delaware to keep this bargain."

"Yes."

Colonel McKee waved a hand toward René LeBlanc, instructing him to unload the sleigh, and the Delawares began counting the provisions. Mary swallowed hard. There was a lump in her throat as she looked at her Indian people. She was proud of them. Hungry as they were and eager to eat, not a sign of it showed on their gaunt, controlled faces. At last the sleigh was empty and it was time to go.

For a second Mary panicked, wishing she had never said she would do it, but one look at the Weasel settled her. With tears in her eyes she hugged Mother Medicine, cast an agonized glance at Little Doe and Cricket, then turned and followed René LeBlanc through the gates of Detroit into her new life.

Chapter 12

DETROIT

The hope of finding Johnny in Detroit had become a fixed idea in Mary's mind, buoying her up through the hardships of the trip. Now as she followed René LeBlanc into the Old Fort this imaginary hope suddenly gave place to stark reality. No smiling brother rushed to greet her, and she was forced to face the fact that the search for him might end in failure.

Her heart was heavy as she stumbled along past a group of wooden barracks into the main thoroughfare of Ste. Anne Street. The narrow road was covered with dirty hard-packed snow and filled with all manner of people. She scanned the faces eagerly for sight of an eleven-year-old boy but the pedestrians were nearly all men — a motley crowd of soldiers, rangers, planters, Indians, half-breeds, fur traders, and voyageurs.

René walked, leading his horse the better to chat with the many friends he met, and Mary had plenty of time to observe the French-style houses which lined both sides of the street. Some were built of log, some of frame but all had high steep roofs in which were set pointed dormer windows indicating a second or even a third floor. Twelve-foot stockade fences surrounded their yards, making them look like miniature forts, and from each house smoke rose from one or two great stone chimneys.

She noticed a musical clamour in the air as if someone were banging on an immense iron drum. René, happening to glance back, caught the puzzled expression on her face and laughing said, "C'est l'église — un mariage."

She had no idea what "L'église" meant but mariage sounded enough like the English word marriage for her to guess that a wedding must be in progress. As they neared the bottom of the street he waved towards a large building on the left from which came the clanging sound. It was a church with a cemetery around it. The wedding guests were pouring out of their wooden sleighs — men in coon coats, women elaborately clothed in fur capes and silk dresses.

They paused for a moment to watch the gay scene then proceeded to the gate in the stockade ahead. "La maison du Gouverneur," murmured René indicating a big house with two full stories on the right. Then they passed through the East Gate and out onto the river front.

Below them lay the King's Wharf with what looked to Mary like a forest of tamarack in a frozen swamp — the masts of dozens of sailing vessels docked for the winter. On the opposite shore of the wide river was an endless row of farm houses surrounded by orchards and outbuildings. Behind them stretched ribbon-like strip farms and, a mile or so beyond, the dark line of the forest.

Part way up that far shore stood what appeared to be another church, and dotted here and there on points of land were queer round towers built of stone and wood, with four immense wings on top of each of them twirling in the wind. They puzzled her. Could they be some kind of lookout stations? It was months before she knew enough French to enquire and discovered that these were the windmills that ground the planter's corn and cut up his planks for flooring.

René led his shaggy pony out onto the frozen river and, climbing into the cariole, motioned for Mary to join him. Just as they were taking off they were hailed from the rear by a loud "Allo René," and another sleigh driven by a lively looking young man drew abreast of them.

"Allo Jacques," responded René and the two men burst into rapid French, the stranger all the time casting admiring glances at Mary. Then gallantly waving his fur cap in the air he bade them good-bye and left.

The pony settled into a steady trot on the frozen river and soon they were beyond the bastion that marked the end of the Old Fort and progressing northward past a continuous row of farm houses. These were built close enough to be within calling distance of each other, and they lined the river's edge like a village street. They had steep roofs like those Mary had seen inside the fort but a few old ones were made of logs stuck upright into the ground like the pickets of a stockaded fort.

René drew rein in front of a dwelling which had been plastered with clay and then whitewashed. He unhitched the pony and, giving it a smart slap on its flank where the letters RL were branded, set it free. Then he pushed open the door of his home and led Mary inside.

They were greeted by Madame LeBlanc, a small dark woman who was rather sickly looking. She smiled a welcome at Mary and then broke into a volley of French. While the LeBlancs talked Mary examined the big kitchen with curiosity. It reminded her vividly of her own old home on Chillisquaque Creek in Pennsylvania. Not for seven years had she been inside a real house with a fireplace for cooking and a table for eating. This house had chairs too, fancy looking chairs with ladder backs and woven rush seats. In one corner was a wooden cupboard and in another a high-backed bench.

With a little cry of joy she sank to her knees beside an iron "spider" frying pan exclaiming, "My mother!"

Madame seemed to understand. "Oui," she said, "ta mère."

It soon became apparent that Madame was displeased with something. She and René were arguing, and Mary was terrified that the woman did not want her and was about to send her back. Finally she realized that it must be the smell of her Indian clothes that was annoying Madame for she held her nose in disgust and turned her head away. Mary remembered how she had once hated that smell herself and she sympathized, but at the same time she had no desire to lose the new doeskin dress and leggings that Mother Medicine had recently made for her.

She objected strenuously when Madame took some of her own clothes from the cupboard and held them out, clutching her doeskin dress to her with such vehemence that René offered to help her. He brought a small wooden chest with a lock and key and indicated that she should put her clothes in it. Then he left her alone with his wife.

Madame made her strip and bathe in a tub of hot sudsy water, washing and combing her hair in search of lice. Mary smiled to herself because she knew she had none. Soon she was scrubbed and dressed in a long blue petticoat over which was a short fawn dress with a white apron and a white cap to match. Her comfortable moccasins were packed away in the little chest with the other things and replaced by knitted socks and hard wooden shoes.

René returned and took Mary with him to see where he was storing the chest on a rafter in a corner of one of his small barns. Then he handed her the key and they returned to the house. In the warm kitchen Madame set her to work stirring something which she called a "pot au feu" which was cooking in a kettle on a crane over the fire. It was a stew of some kind, Mary knew by the smell, and she could hardly wait to eat.

What a thrill it gave her to again see someone set a table for a meal with bowls and pewter spoons. Although these people were not her own, they roused memories of her own family and the heartbreak that had lain dormant for many years.

After supper when she had time to look around she noticed a second room opening off the kitchen from beside the fireplace. It contained something that she had heard about as a child but had never seen before — a four-poster bed. That must be where René and Madame slept. But where was she to sleep?

A miracle took place at bedtime. With an adroit twist of his strong right hand René jerked the seat of the bench, or banc-lit as he called it, toward him and it opened out into a large box filled with straw. Madame added a couple of quilts and they left Mary there to sleep.

As she curled up in comfort in her box-bed her thoughts wandered off into the forest, where she knew Mother Medicine, Little Doe and all her Delaware family and friends were filling their empty stomachs with the food she had provided.

Chapter 13

CARIOLE FUN

Mary had plenty of work to do and many things to learn, such as how to milk cows and how to carry two buckets of water at a time from the river using a yoke on her shoulders to steady them. The floor of the LeBlanc house was laid with wide pine boards and the cracks between them were filled with earth, necessitating frequent sweeping. Besides the cooking and washing there were chickens and pigs to feed and a woodbox to keep filled.

In the evenings the LeBlancs relaxed. Neighbours came to call – the Chauvin family from next door, a father and mother with four of their large family, two sons, Armand and Antoine and two vivacious daughters, Thérèse and Joséphine. The Tremblay family from the other side were also frequent visitors, and with them came their cousin, Jacques Brandon, the young man whom Mary had met the first day with René on the river. He was a British soldier, half French so she learned later, and a serjeant in one of the regiments of the garrison.

Mary knew they were all curious about her and could tell when they were discussing her, even though she could not understand the words. Once she heard René say "Américaine."

"No," she contradicted him promptly, "British –

King George."

"Ah! Breeteesh, eh? Le roi Georges. Detroit Bree-teesh."

Mary nodded. She knew that. Jacques then tried to draw her out in English. "Where are you from?" he asked.

"Pennsylvania, Shamokin." Launched on the old memory lesson that she had tried so hard to drill into Johnny, she now gave it all to them in one breath: "I was born in New Jersey. My father was Peter Whitmore and he was killed at Shamokin in Pennsylvania on Easter Day in 1780."

Jacques translated this into French for the others who nodded sympathetically. But try as he would he could not get her to say any more. She had forgotten her English. None but Delaware words came to her mind.

Antoine Chauvin always brought his fiddle with him in the evenings for singing and dancing. At first Mary shrank shyly into a corner, refusing to take part in the gaiety, but eventually, as she made friends with Thérèse and Joséphine, she learned their songs, joined in the dancing and accompanied the LeBlancs on return visits to the neighbouring homes.

On Sunday the habitant families set forth in their carioles for church, forming a solemn procession on the frozen river to Ste Anne's in the Old Fort. Mary could hear the bell ringing long before they reached their destination. As she entered the church a wave of warm air perfumed with incense and pungent with the odour of evergreen boughs met her nostrils. Her keen blue eyes took in every detail of the scene, the tall altar candles, the statues and vestments and the clothes of the congregation. The intoning of the priest reminded her of the impressive cadences of the Delawares when they met in the Council House, the only difference being that here one man seemed to do all the talking – no one answered him! On their way out she saw Jacques in his scarlet uniform standing at the back of the church with others from his regiment, and she returned the smile he gave her.

The surprise of the day for Mary was the cariole race. They had driven down river sedately enough on their way to church but going home was a different matter. All the sleighs lined up on the ice and at the crack of a pistol set off on a mad race amid the excited shouts of the drivers. Madame and Mary huddled under the bearskin rug to avoid the stinging wind and clung to each other for dear life. Faster and faster they went until only three contestants remained in the lead: René, Chauvin and another man. Then the Chauvin cariole drew ahead to win the weekly race.

One day a few months later the Chauvin girls arrived in a fever of excitement. The cariole dance, they said, was to be held the following Saturday in their home. The LeBlancs were equally excited when they heard this news and Mary, who could now speak a little French, asked what a cariole dance was.

Once a week all winter on Saturdays, the girls explained it was the custom for the young men and ladies from Detroit, the officers and their wives, the fur merchants and their daughters, and anyone else who was interested, to plan a dance and dinner party at some farm on the river. The men came armed with two plates, two forks and two glasses each. The married men provided the meat and the single ones the wine. The host family and their neighbours not only attended the party but also did a profitable business supplying butter, milk and other necessities. The guests drove out on the river ice in their carioles, about thirty of them, in an orderly procession with music at the head. They arrived at noon, danced until three, ate until five and then drove off again in their sleighs.

Officers! Here at last was the opportunity Mary had been longing for – a chance to enquire about Johnny. She prepared questions in French ahead of time and learned them by heart.

The Chauvin kitchen was large but even so they had quite a time to make room for so many guests. The men pushed the furniture against the wall or moved it into other rooms; the women cleaned, polished and cooked, and everything was ready when the great day arrived – clear, cold and sparkling.

They could hear the music and sleigh bells while they were still a great way off – and the gay singing. Soon the house was filled with laughter, with scarlet uniforms and bright coloured silks, with gartered breeches and snowy white jabots. Mary had never seen such grandeur before. She was awestruck as she and Joséphine Chauvin perched on a pile of upturned benches in a corner to watch the fun.

"That is Captain Thomas McKee of the 60th Regiment over there," whispered Joséphine. "He is a son of Colonel McKee and he is talking to his fiancée Thérèse Askin. She's the daughter of John Askin, the wealthy fur merchant."

The fiddlers were tuning up for the first dance as Mary answered, "I know Colonel McKee. He was the one who arranged for me to live with the LeBlancs."

"And there," continued Joséphine, "is Jacques Baby's son Jacques. They call him Jacques Baby Mini. His father is a great man here, the spokesman for all our French people, and he has twenty-two children."

"Goodness!" said Mary, "there were ten in my

family and we thought that was a lot."

At this point the Chauvin boys persuaded the two girls to join in the dance and it was not until later that Mary had a chance to enquire about Johnny. She happened to be standing next to her friend Jacques Brandon so she asked him, "Is the Governor here?"

"We have had no governor in Detroit for a year. We are under military rule now and Major Ancrum, standing over there beside the chimney, is in command."

"Will you please introduce me to him Jacques? I want to ask him to help me find my brother."

"No, not I. Serjeants and majors just don't mix. If you want to talk to him you will have to do it on your own."

Mary was disappointed that Jacques refused to help her but this was her big chance and she was determined to make the most of it for Johnny's sake. Bracing herself, she shyly approached the major.

"Please, sir. Could you help me find my brother? His name is John Whitmore and he is eleven years old. I think he lives with a British officer in Detroit."

"I never heard of him. No British officer in Detroit has a boy of that name. Perhaps he is in one of the other British forts – at Michilimackinac or Erie, Niagara or Oswego, Chambly or even in Montreal. He is not here."

Mary's face must have shown her deep disappointment for he added kindly, "Go and ask Colonel Alexander McKee, the Superintendant of Indian Affairs. He knows more about Indian captives than anyone. Tell him I sent you."

"Yes, Sir. Thank you."

So there was no hope left of finding Johnny in

Detroit! And how could she possibly go to all those other forts in search of him? Three hundred miles northwest to Michilimackinac, six hundred miles east to Montreal – it was impossible. As for Colonel McKee, she knew that his plantation or farm was some distance away at the mouth of the Detroit River below the fort.

Later when she told her troubles to the LeBlancs – Madame surprised her by saying, "René has to take a load of wood to town for the garrison on Monday. Why don't you go with him and after his business is done he will drive you down to Colonel McKee's."

At Colonel McKee's they found his spacious grounds filled with Butler's Rangers and Indians of many tribes – Wyandottes, Ottawas, Pottawatomies, Chippewas and a few Shawnees. Mary searched in vain for a Delaware face.

Suddenly, as she and René were walking towards the large house past a group of lounging Indians, she found herself looking straight into the sly, evil face of de Coignée. For one second as their eyes met she saw a spark of recognition in his, and then he melted out of sight behind the other men and was gone.

White faced Mary gripped René's arm.

"What's wrong?" he asked.

"I just saw the man who murdered my father and he knew me!"

A ranger now came forward to show them into McKee's office and there was no time to say more. Colonel McKee recognized them at once and asked René why they had come. René indicated that Mary wished to speak to him and she, knowing the Colonel understood Delaware, spoke up freely and fluently, explaining that Major Ancrum had sent her to him, that she was in search of Johnny and that she needed his help. The Colonel stood there aloof and apparently indifferent in his gold-laced uniform until she had finished. Then he said, "Hundreds and hundreds of Indian captives have passed through Detroit in the last ten years. We can not possibly keep track of them. I never heard of your brother. I can do nothing for you."

Desperation gave Mary courage. "But you have heard of a man out there in your yard called de Coignée, haven't you?"

"Of course. He is one of my interpreters."

"Well, he must know where my sister Sarah Whitmore and my brothers Peter and George are, for he was with them when the Senecas took them away captive. Besides he is a traitor and is probably acting as a spy in your camp."

McKee's indifference vanished. He snapped an order at the attendant ranger, "Get de Coignée."

When the ranger had gone he turned to Mary. "What evidence have you that de Coignée is a traitor?"

"I was present when he killed my father in the spring of 1780. He was with a gang of revolutionaries that day. Before then he fought for the British. My father, who knew him well always said he was not to be trusted, that he fought first for one side and then for the other."

The ranger returned saying that de Coignée had disappeared and McKee turned to Mary, "You think he recognized you?"

"I know he did."

"Then he may have felt it wiser to decamp before I started making enquiries about him. I've suspected for some time that he was doublecrossing me." And the Colonel indicated that the interview was over. But just as

Mary and René reached the door he spoke again. "If I hear any news of your family, Miss Whitmore, I will let you know."

It was a cold and dreary drive home. "Don't despair, Marie," said René kindly. "Some day you will find your brother."

When the wild geese flew north and the ice in the river began to crack Mary felt cooped up in the house. She missed the freedom of her Indian home and looked with longing at the distant line of forest. "It is the moon of maple sugar," she said.

"Not moon Marie, month – the month of March," corrected René.

"It's a moon to me," she answered with a sigh that expressed homesick longing for her Delaware family and their life in the open.

Madame was expecting a baby and to Mary's trained eye she looked ill and in need of the specialized care that she and Mother Medicine had so often given to the Indian women on the Allegheny. The doctor from the garrison came but did little except prescribe rest.

René was dejected. Five times, so he told Mary, they had lost their babies. He was afraid that this time he might lose Madame as well.

"Not if she were a Delaware woman. Mother Medicine taught me the herbs to use to prevent this sort of thing."

"Well, we'll see. You and I can go to the forest and get the herbs you require and then if the doctor can't do anything perhaps Madame will let you help her."

Mary agreed but she was afraid if Madame left it so long it might be too late for the Delaware treatment to take effect. She went with René to the forest and collected the necessary herbs which she then dried and stored in one of the outbuildings.

Spring came on with a rush; bluebirds and robins sang in the budding trees and the damp earth gave forth its good rich odour as the sun beat down on ploughed fields. In May the whole Detroit River became a thing of beauty – apple, pear, peach and plum blossoms made frothy clouds of pink and white between the old farm homes. In the evenings the young people now took their fiddles out of doors and danced or promenaded under the trees, while their parents gossiped contentedly on the doorsteps or sat watching the passing ships.

Jacques and Mary paused under the LeBlanc's big pear tree. "What makes it grow so much bigger than all the others?" she asked.

"I don't know. All the pear trees here do. This one is about eighty feet high. Our grandparents brought them from their homes on the St. Lawrence. Originally the trees came over with their ancestors from Normandy, but I've heard it said that even in Quebec and Normandy the pear trees did not grow as big as they do here."

"It's wonderful," said Mary, gazing up into the soft white above them.

Jacques broke off a branch of blossoms and gave it to her. "We could have a farm and a tree like this of our own, Marie, if you would marry me. Will you marry me?"

Mary was surprised and confused. She had never thought of marrying Jacques. He was just a good friend and jolly companion. She hesitated and then stammered, "Oh, Jacques I don't know. Could you please give me time to think about it?"

Jacques looked hurt. "Very well," he said, "until tomorrow evening."

Chapter 14

HER TWELFTH MOON

Should she marry Jacques and settle down in the French farming community of Detroit? Give up her search for Johnny? Give up hope of finding Sarah and the others? This was Mary's problem. Marriage to Jacques would provide a safe existence instead of the uncertain future that now faced her. But she had contracted to work twelve moons for René LeBlanc and seven of those moons had already passed. When the twelfth moon was up what was then to become of her?

Mary's own plan was to go in search of Johnny, to every fort in British North America if necessary. The idea of marriage had not entered her head and she hardly felt as close to Jacques Brandon as she had to Fleet Foot and that closeness, she now realized on looking back, was only a passing attraction. Her mind travelled back still further to her childhood friends – to the Welliver and Billhime boys, to her cousin Bill Sheets and his friend Henry Hoople with the laughing blue eyes. She knew it would be foolishness to hope to meet any of them again after all these years. They might have been killed in the Revolutionary War or, if spared, were all probably married by now. However the memory of them did serve as a sort of yardstick by which to evaluate other men, and somehow she felt Jacques did not quite measure up to it.

She gave him her decision the next evening under the giant pear tree in as kind a way as possible, explaining that her whole life was dedicated to the search for her lost family.

Life was dull after that. She missed having Jacques for her partner at the parties when the other young people paired off, and she was amused to see how soon he began paying attention to Joséphine Chauvin. She soon found she preferred to stay home from the parties and take refuge in work.

With Madame ill all the household and barnyard chores fell on Mary's shoulders, for René was busy from sunup to sunset in the fields. All of them were tired enough by evening to retire early or to sit quietly on the doorstep watching the river traffic.

The river was their lifeline. On its ice they drove their carioles to town in winter and over its smooth surface paddled their small canoes in summer. After a hot day's work they looked to the river for a cool breeze and found in its busy shipping an unfailing source of entertainment.

When there was a wind the canvas-covered arms of the big windmills on the far shore twisted and turned in the breeze, while nearer to them in the deep channel the great white sails of ships billowed out in graceful curves, and on moonlit nights the music of young people in their canoes singing the old French songs floated to them over the water.

"That big vessel over there," said René one evening, "is His Majesty's brig *Gage*, built right here in Detroit in our own shipyard. The British Governor ordered nine battleships built to protect the town and she is the biggest of them. One hundred and fifty-four tons she is and carries fourteen guns. Beyond her is another of them, the schooner *Hope,* and way off there to the left near Isle Aux Cochons is the smallest of the nine, the sloop *Adventure.*

"They were expecting an attack then?" queried Mary.

"Yes, and they still do. All this summer the soldiers of the garrison have been mending the stockade of the Old Fort and deepening the moat around the new one." As he finished speaking they were startled by the distant boom of cannon.

Mary turned wide-eyed to René, "Is that an attack now?"

"No, I hardly think so – more likely a scalp parade."

"A scalp parade here? We had those in my Delaware village," she said shuddering at the memory. "It was part of the Indian tradition. But here? Surely not here in a British fort?"

"Yes. The Indian tribes around here are our allies. When they bring in scalps after a victory the commander fires the cannon to show appreciation for their efforts, and for the same reason allows them to parade their scalps and prisoners through the streets. Sometimes we French planters go to the Commons and rescue the prisoners from torture."

"Don't forget," he continued, "the British and Americans are still at war here and on the Ohio. That peace they signed a few years ago at Versailles to end the Revolutionary War did not end hostilities west of the Alleghenies. American settlers continue to pour over the mountains into the forests needed by the British for the fur trade but it seems as hopeless to stop them as to try to dam up Niagara. Soon I think we will give up. Meantime we fight – the battle of the beaver!"

As Madame's time drew near she became very ill indeed and René went once more to the fort to fetch the garrison doctor. He came but only shook his head. "You will be lucky," he said to René, "if your wife survives this time. I can do nothing."

Madame overheard this conversation and called Mary to her. "If you think you can help me with your Indian medicine I wish you would try but I want to have Geneviève, the midwife, here too."

"I will do my best, Madame. Have Geneviève if you wish but only if she agrees to the Indian method. I will need to have a free hand."

Madame and René both agreed to this arrangement, and Mary went at once to the shed for the herbs and roots that she had stored there in the spring. She began by dosing Madame with a special concoction of bark from the root of the black haw mixed with pearly everlasting and bayberry to build up her blood. Then she carefully explained the Delaware medicine to her.

"There are three parts to it," she said. "First there are herbs and roots from the forest, tried and proven by generations of Indians: a tonic of grape vine, peppermint and sarsaparilla, to give you strength, and bloodroot to make the birth itself easier and to make milk for the baby when it arrives. In the second place we recommend a special position. Instead of the mother lying down we encourage her to walk around and to take the natural position of kneeling for the birth itself. This makes it easier and safer for both the mother and the baby. Finally, and this is the most important thing, both the mother and the doctor ask the Great Spirit for help and trust that he will answer their prayers."

A few days later when Madame was in labour with

both Mary and Geneviève in attendance, René sat alone by the chimney bowed over with anxiety, his head in his hand. He hardly knew whether he dared to hope or not. Suddenly he heard above the other sounds that came from the next room a high thin wail that startled and thrilled him. Could it be? – Could it possibly be?

Mary slipped in beside him and placed a bundle in his arms – "Your son, René."

"My – my – son? Is it possible that he is born and lives?"

"Yes, indeed, Look!" she drew back the covers and showed him a tiny red and crinkled face.

René trembled so much he almost dropped the precious bundle. "And what – of Madame?" he asked.

"She is very weak but living. I must return to her now," said Mary taking the baby with her to show to his mother.

"You have a beautiful big boy," she said to Madame, holding the baby up so she could see him. Madame opened her eyes with an effort as if she had come back from a long way off. "You must get strong so you can nurse him."

A tiny smile flickered on Madame's face for a second and then her eyelids closed again, but her breathing was steadier and stronger from then on.

Geneviève stayed with them for a week until Madame began to gain strength and then she went home to spread the news up and down the river. "Madame LeBlanc has a baby son – at last, after losing five. After the garrison doctor gave up all hope that Whitmore girl doctored her the Indian way and both mother and child are alive and well!"

Mary was so busy after that she had no time to think at all, and the weeks and the months passed quickly – August, September, October.

One fine day in late October a canoe paddled by two of Butler's Rangers landed at their wharf and out of it stepped a strange man – tall, fair, red-faced and very dignified."

"My name is Pastor Schmidt of the Lutheran Church," he said to René in French that was heavily weighted with a thick German accent. "I am searching for a girl named Whitmore and Colonel McKee told me I might find her here."

Mary came in just then carrying René Mini as they called the baby. "This is Marie Whitmore," said René. "Marie, this man – Pastor Schmidt – has some news of your family."

"Johnny?" breathed Mary, her eyes shining.

"No – Jacob," said the stranger.

"My brother Jake?" she could hardly say the words she was so excited.

"No, not a brother. This man is old. Jacob Schütz or Sheets is his name."

"Jacob Sheets is my uncle – my mother's brother."

"Yes, so I gather. I held a Lutheran service in his home last summer and afterwards he told me about the massacre of his sister in Pennsylvania. He asked me to help him locate her children by enquiring for them wherever I went in my travels. He begged me to send them to him if I found any of them."

"Where is he?"

"He lives about five hundred miles east of here on the Long Sault Rapids in the St. Lawrence River between

Cataraqui and Montreal. He fought for the King in the Revolutionary War in the King's Royal Regiment of New York, and afterwards received a grant of land there for his loyalty."

"His son Bill visited us once in Pennsylvania but he said his father was in the 'Royal Greens'."

"Well, yes. That is the same thing. The Royal Greens was a nickname for the King's Royal Regiment of New York."

Pastor Schmidt left them then, saying he would make arrangements to take Mary with him to her uncle when he again left for the east.

"My own people!" exclaimed Mary, after he had gone. "At last I have found someone of my own." It was disappointing to have no word of Johnny but an uncle who wanted her was the next best thing. She was so thrilled she dashed next door to tell the Chauvin girls the news.

About a month later Pastor Schmidt appeared once more on the doorstep. "I leave tomorrow for the east," he said, "Are you ready to go with me?"

"Oh no! I can't do that!" exclaimed Mary in deep distress. "I am bound out to René LeBlanc for twelve moons and I have only worked eleven."

"The last fur brigade canoe going east leaves tomorrow. It is the end of navigation before freeze up. You must go now or not at all."

It was a cruel choice. Mary was white-faced but firm as she answered, "I gave my word as a Delaware before Colonel McKee and the Chief and braves of my tribe that I would serve twelve moons, and serve twelve moons I must."

While she was speaking René had left the room. He returned now with something in his hand. Walking up to Mary he gave it to her – a leaf folded and tied with red yarn like a parcel. "For you, Marie," he said.

She untied it carefully until the leaf lay flat on her hand, open – and empty!

"What is it?" she asked, surprised.

"That is your twelfth moon," he said. "You are not the only one who believes in fair play. You owe me a month yes, but I owe you more than I can ever repay – the life of my wife and son. Go tomorrow, Marie, with our blessing."

Chapter 15

THE VOYAGEURS

The sun was breaking through early morning mists as René paddled Mary up to the Merchant's Dock. Quite a crowd had gathered there including the Commander of the Fort, the priest from Ste. Anne's and the wealthy fur merchant, John Askin, who did business for the North West Company. The departure of the final fur brigade of the season was always an important event in Detroit, providing the citizens with their last chance to send mail east to Montreal before they were isolated by the long winter.

René lifted Mary's chest onto the wharf and helped her to scramble up beside it, then left her to moor his craft. Her heart beat high as she gazed at the huge thirty-six foot canoe drawn up on the opposite side of the dock, ready and waiting to carry her into a new adventure. Its high curved ends showed above the edge of the wharf and from the prow hung a small flag on which were the letters NWCo. Behind it rose a tangle of masts and rigging made by sailing vessels beached for the winter, and beyond them stretched the stockaded walls of the Old Fort.

Conspicuous in the crowd were the ten voyageurs who were going to man the big canoe. Small men, dark and wiry with broad shoulders, they stood around nonchalantly smoking their shortstemmed pipes. Coloured stocking-caps trimmed with feathers and a tassel were set at jaunty angles over their ears, and around their waists were tied red woven sashes. Proud, and with reason, of their strength and skill in a demanding occupation, they swaggered a little when they moved. Each of them held in his hand a paddle, his personal property, carved out of basswood by himself and painted to his own taste.

Mary examined the voyageurs with interest for she was about to put her life in their hands on a journey of five hundred miles. Then she noticed that they in turn were examining her. She had thought she would remain unnoticed in the crowd, not realizing that the men had been told they were to have a lady passenger and obviously she, standing alone beside her little chest with Madame's crimson shawl wrapped around her shoulders and a blue kerchief tied over her tawny-coloured hair, must be the one.

René returned to say goodbye as Antoine Chauvin

arrived breathless, his arms full of packages. "For your uncle from Madame LeBlanc", he said, "pemmican and hard tack that will keep on the journey. Madame heard that the settlers in the East are starving. Here, let me help you pack them."

Mary knelt to open her chest. Hardly had she locked it again when it was time to go and Pastor Schmidt came to hurry her over to the big canoe. All the men but one were already kneeling in their places with paddles raised. The bowman swung Mary's chest aboard and handed her to her seat in the centre between Pastor Schmidt and a gaunt man in a tall beaver hat whom she learned later was Mr. MacDonald, the company agent. The bowman then took his place and the steersman in the stern, half-kneeling half-standing, pushed off.

Ten gaily painted paddles dipped in the water as one and then were raised glistening in the sunlight in a parting salute. The crowd shouted "Bon voyage," and then fell silent for the moment of benediction. The paddles dipped again in earnest and they were off.

There was a commotion behind them on the dock and Mary, glancing back, saw a red-coated figure hurtle through the crowd, fling both arms into the air and shout, "Adieu Marie, bon voyage!" It was Jacques, irrepressible as usual. She smiled and waved, then turned to admire the scenery of the Lower Straits. How she hated the pain of these partings – first from her own family, then from her Delaware family and now from her French friends.

They moved swiftly past a long line of settled farms, a windmill and the last of the islands, the voyageurs paddling to the rhythm of their own songs while the company flag fluttered from the prow.

"Fort Malden," said Mr. MacDonald, jerking his head to the left where stood a small fort, "built agin the day we maun gie Detroit to the Yankees."

"Butler's Rangers," he said a little later as they came out into the shining open waters of Lake Erie. He indicated clearings and new log homes which lined the north shore of the lake for a short distance. "They are keerful tae build on the richt side o'the water."

Mary caught the words "Butler's Rangers" and looked at the English style houses with interest but she could not understand the language in which her fellow passengers conversed. Now and again Pastor Schmidt translated an item for her in his heavily accented French but for the most part she had to amuse herself by listening to the songs of the Canadiens.

"En roulant ma boule, roulant," chanted Jacquot, the song leader.

"En roulant ma boule," replied the crew.

"En roulant ma boule, roulant," they all sang together and Mary, who had learned that song at the LeBlanc's sang with them. Hour after hour they paddled and sang.

"Pipes!" came the clear command of Pépin, the steersman. Suddenly all paddling stopped as every man lit his pipe and flexed his muscles, glad of the traditional short rest period.

By nightfall they had covered about forty miles and made camp in a sheltered cove on the north shore, a "pipe place" apparently well known to the men. The canoe came to a standstill some distance from land and all the men jumped waist-deep into the water. Then, while the steersman and bowman steadied the craft, each of the passengers was lifted onto the shoulders of a voyageur and carried pick-a-back to shore.

The sight of the stern Scot and dignified pastor in midair was too much for Mary. She giggled. Pastor Schmidt was indignant. Red-faced he spluttered, "They always do this, as a courtesy to their passengers."

The Scot shook himself in disgust as he was set down on the sand. "I'd prefair tae wade in," he said, "an nae mak sic a fool o'mesel but they hae their rules and maun obey them."

From long habit on Delaware trails Mary set to work at once to gather wood for the fire but she was reproved by Pépin. "Leave it to the men. It is their job."

Soon a pot of parched corn and fat pork was bubbling over the campfire and while they ate the men vied with each other in telling jokes and tall tales of their exploits, singing and laughing uproariously.

Mary was then given the place of honour beside the fire and left alone there to sleep rolled up in her blanket. She felt at home outdoors under the stars listening to the familiar night sounds of the forest and the soft lapping of waves on the shore. She lay and gazed up at the Big Bear the way she and Little Doe had often done on the Allegheny and wondered if her friend were watching it now too. And what of Mother Medicine? Had she followed her husband to the Happy Hunting Grounds as she had prophesied? Her thoughts trailed off gradually and she was lulled to sleep by her uncle the West Wind sighing in the pines.

"Lève!" Like a pistol shot the command of Pépin rang out. They started before daylight and without breakfast. The disembarking process of the night before was repeated in reverse and the men, wet to the waist, climbed into the canoe while Mr. MacDonald, whose job it was to supervise the use of rum during the trip, doled out a tot to each of them to avoid chills.

Two hours later they landed again and built a fire for breakfast – the same menu as before, a mess of corn and pork. "This is why voyageurs are called 'pork eaters'," said Pastor Schmidt downing his portion with noisy gusto.

Two meals a day was the rule and always the same food but sometimes at noon the men broke off a hunk of uncooked pemmican to chew while they paddled. To Mary, who had experienced near starvation on the Allegheny, two hearty meals a day seemed plentiful.

She could tell without asking which of the men were part Indian and was drawn to them from the first. Somehow they sensed this and responded. As she grew to know them better she learned all their names and where they came from. Pépin, the steersman and boss, was from Montreal; Jean, the bowman came from Trois Rivières; Etienne and Jules were from Lachine; Jacquot, the song leader, and his brother Michel were from Sorel; Bepo was from Longueuil and Josèphe, an older man, from Cap de la Madeleine.

The men were pleased that Mary bothered to call each of them by name. Homeward bound their minds were already racing ahead, visualizing the girl next door or the old grandmother in her rocking chair beneath the prie-dieu. They welcomed the chance to talk of their home towns, silently blessing Mary for caring enough to enquire about them, and by evening of the third day they had drawn from her the story of her captivity and search for her sister and brothers.

"Tomorrow night," said Pépin, "we camp near the mouth of the Grand where the Six Nations have their lands. Some of us can paddle you up river to call on Chief Joseph Brant of the Mohawks."

"Oh, that would be wonderful," Mary knew there

were Senecas with Brant on the Grand and she hoped they might be able to give her news of Sarah. However, the main plan was to enquire for Johnny among the British officers in Fort Niagara.

"We do go to Fort Niagara, don't we?" she asked anxiously. "Yes. We go by it," replied Pépin vaguely, not realizing that she meant did they actually go right into the fort. He did not know how important this matter was to her.

On the Grand they met only a few Cayugas who told them that Brant, accompanied by most of the braves, had gone to the great Indian conference beyond Detroit and had not yet returned. Mary was disappointed but only mildly so because her main hope was of finding Johnny at Fort Niagara which still lay ahead of them.

Late the next afternoon they passed Fort Erie on their left, a group of fortified buildings perched on a stone wall at the water's edge where the lake begins to empty itself into the Niagara River. Several schooners lay near the fort, the British flag flew from its ramparts and, beyond it on the west bank of the river stretched a ragged line of clearings dotted with log houses and burnt stumps. All this they ignored and turning instead towards the thickly forested east bank, they floated downsteam for several miles to Fort Schlosser. This consisted of a large house with an immense chimney surrounded by orchards and outbuildings.

"It looks more like a farm than a fort," observed Mary.

"That's just what it is," answered Pastor Schmidt. "John Stedman is the Portage Master and it is his farm. He built his house around the chimney of the old fort which was destroyed some years ago. You will notice there are no other farms on this side of the river because this is Seneca country and they won't allow any settlement but in reparation for the Devil's Hole Massacre, the Senecas allow portage rights to the British. Mr. Stedman was one of three men who escaped alive from that horror. We must ask him to tell you the story tonight."

"Does he speak French?"

"Yes and Seneca too. You and I and Mr. MacDonald will be spending the night with him while the men take the canoe and cargo down to the Lower Landing. They will leave most of the cargo here in safe keeping in Mr. Stedman's storehouses and come back for it in the morning. Then while they are carrying it down we three can follow the trail at our leisure, with time to see the Falls on the way by."

Mary was distressed. She did not care particularly about seeing the Falls but she was in a fever to reach Fort Niagara and make enquiries there for Johnny. She was trying to explain this to the pastor when Mr. Stedman came out to welcome them and she had no further chance to speak of it.

She watched with professional interest the unloading of the 4000 pound cargo and preparations for carrying it down the twelve-mile trail. Among the Delaware Mary had been considered an expert on a portage, sometimes carrying as much as a hundred pounds, and she longed now to use her skill to help the men with their task.

Noticing her concern Mr. Stedman spoke to her kindly. "Don't worry about them, Miss. They pride themselves on how much they can carry and if they manage more than two of those ninety-pound bundles at a time they receive extra pay."

Mr. Stedman fed them a real dinner of fish with

vegetables and fruit from his farm, serving Madeira wine to the gentlemen and a mug of goat's milk to Mary.

"Goats?" queried Mary. "I'd love to see them."

"They are not here, my dear. I keep them on an island near the Falls so they will be safe from wolves. I have to go over in a bateau every time I want milk. You will probably see them as you go by tomorrow."

In the evening as they sat around a blazing fire Pastor Schmidt persuaded Mr. Stedman to describe his experience in the Devil's Hole Massacre.

"The Senecas were angry," he began. "They had given the British the right of portage through their lands in return for the privilege of carrying the loads for pay. When the British suddenly took their job away from them, hiring white truckers with carts and oxen in their stead, the Senecas decided to take revenge. They lay in ambush near a high cliff above the river, and when a train of twenty-five wagons came along with drivers, oxen, a hundred horses and an accompanying detachment of twenty-four soldiers, they pushed the whole lot over the cliff. Only three of us came out of that mess alive. I managed to jump on a horse and escape. One wounded soldier crawled under a bush and was not seen by the Indians, and a drummer boy fell into the branches of a tree which saved him from being crushed like the others on the rocks below. The green waters of the Niagara ran red that day, and ever since that part of the river has been called the Bloody Run."

The roar of the great cataracts thundered in their ears next morning as Mary and the two men descended the Portage Trail. She wished they would hurry. She could hardly wait to get to Fort Niagara. She had slept little all night for thinking about Johnny. But the men insisted on taking their time, ambling down a side trail through the forest to a spot from which they could show her the Falls, as well as the island on which grazed Mr. Stedman's goats. Later they stopped again to point out the Devil's Hole and the Bloody Run.

At last they reached the Lower Landing where a blockhouse and several storehouses stood on a high bank. From there a track led down to the green water below, where the canoe waited loaded and ready to leave. There was no sign at all of Fort Niagara.

"We must leave at once," said Pépin. "There is bad weather brewing."

"But Fort Niagara?" stammered Mary, "Where is it?"

"We will pass it as we go out into Lake Ontario."

"Pass it! No. No! I must go there to ask for my brother," she wailed.

"You go, Miss, if you wish, but you go alone. We leave at once to cross to the north shore of the lake before the storm breaks."

Mary stood still in horror. What a terrible decision to have to make! What should she do?

Pastor Schmidt laid a firm hand on her shoulder. "You have no choice. You are in my care. I undertook to deliver you to your uncle and I say we go – and now."

There was no questioning his authority. Sick at heart she slipped into the canoe and sank in a heap between the two men, thinking bitterly of the time wasted in viewing the Falls, blaming herself for not having spoken up and insisted on hurrying.

"I didna ken the lassie wanted sae sair to go to Fort Niagara," said Mr. MacDonald, "but there wouldna hae been time tae mak it there and back. Overland it is three leagues frae here to the Fort."

The pastor translated this for Mary in his halting French and added on his own, "You are not really certain your brother is there. He may not be. If he is you can always come back some day and find him."

This was cold comfort to Mary. She slumped in an agony of remorse. If only she had known in time that they would not pass through the famous Fort on the way to the Lower Landing. She was filled with an intuitive feeling that Johnny was here somewhere near her and that every stroke of the paddles was carrying her farther and farther away from him. At the thought all the stiffening went out of her neck and her head drooped on her chest.

The men felt badly. Those in front kept looking back at her in distress. They tried all her favorite songs one after another in hopes of rousing her – but in vain.

"Yonder's Fort Niagara," said Mr. MacDonald, pointing to a rocky promontory on their right crowned by a group of large stone buildings above which flew the flag of Britain.

Mary roused herself long enough to look at it with glazed eyes. She had expected it to be similar to Detroit, a stockaded town enclosing hundreds of houses, stores and a church. Instead it was only a grim fortress. It hardly seemed likely that her brother would be inside it. She sank back again on her seat.

Chapter 16

WHITE WATER

Lake Ontario lay before them as far as the eye could see, bluer and darker than Lake Erie except that a brown streak reached out into the blue from the lefthand shore where a small stream emptied its mud into the lake. This caught Mary's eye and she sat up, fascinated. At that moment her intuitive feeling that Johnny was near her became stronger and she felt that he was in some way connected with the stream. But, alas, the relentless paddles dipped and dipped, and soon the brown patch was left far behind. She slumped again.

The next time she looked up all was grey – endless grey sky, grey water and a matching grey of despair in herself. She had not realized until then that her main purpose in going east had been to search for Johnny. The spark of excitement with which she had begun the journey was now gone and her spirits sagged.

"C'est la belle Françoise, bon gai," sang the voyageurs, hoping to cheer her. Jacquot turned to look at her and she smiled at him sadly but could not bring herself to sing.

"The Little One is wounded and can't sing," muttered Jacquot.

"Try 'Lizette'," answered Bepo. "She likes that one."

"La belle Lizette chantait l'autre jour," sang Jacquot.

"La chantait l'autre jour," responded the crew, but Mary never even lifted her head.

Pépin was worried, not because he had refused to wait over for her to go to Fort Niagara, that had been his duty. The lives of thirteen people and a valuable cargo were in his care and he knew that a day lost so late in November might mean they would find the St. Lawrence frozen and unnavigable before they reached Montreal. What did worry Pépin was the men's reaction. They were unhappy because the Little One was unhappy and consequently they were not putting their best into the paddling. This might prove fatal in an emergency.

Large whitecaps began to top the waves, curling over on themselves in frothy masses. The wind howled past their ears with blizzard strength and in the distance were ominous growls of thunder. "Try 'La Canadienne'," ordered Pépin.

"Vive la Canadienne, vole ma coeur, vole," chanted Jacquot.

"Vive la Canadienne et ses jolis yeux doux," replied the crew and all the men in the front turned to see whether Mary responded.

She felt their eyes on her, beseeching, and letting go her own pain, she lifted her head and made a valiant effort to oblige them. "Et ses jolis yeux doux," she warbled tremulously.

"Vive la Canadienne," shouted the men with glee and their paddles dug deeper into the mounting waves.

"Mon Dieu," exclaimed Pépin, "but I am thankful. Now we will be all right."

Jagged forks of lightning stabbed the sky and the thunder rolled closer. Rain fell at first in great drops that bounced back off the surface of the waves and then in blinding sheets which threatened to fill the canoe. The pastor and the agent bailed, the crew sang and paddled for their lives and Mary, forgetting her own problem, sang and bailed with them.

"Land!" shouted Jean joyfully as ahead of them appeared a massive bed of reeds and rushes.

"It is the mouth of the Credit River," said Josèphe.

The rain ceased and the sun came out between parting clouds as they pushed their way through the rushes to a high sandy bank and landed there in a grove of oaks. Like everyone else Mary was drenched so she rigged up a tent by wrapping a wet blanket around two saplings and changed out of Madame's soaking clothes into her own Indian doeskins which were dry inside her chest. When she emerged she found every available branch hung with coloured shirts, blankets and soaked beaver pelts. The men too had changed into clothes which had kept dry in waterproof rolls.

It seemed to Mary that nothing had ever tasted better than the hot corn and pork they cooked that night. While they were eating a canoeload of Mississaugas appeared through the rushes. They had seen smoke and came to investigate. Josèphe, who had spent much of his youth in the fur trade along this shore and could speak the Mississauga tongue, acted as interpreter.

To Mary's enquiries they answered that they had no white prisoners and knew no British officers. They said they were a quiet people minding their own business, hunting and fishing in the hinterland to the north and coming out to the river's mouth only to grow corn on the good bottom lands and to trade.

"That," explained Josèphe, "is how this river got its name. In the old days our French traders met the Indians here in the Fall, giving them credit in advance for the furs they hoped to get the following winter. The Indians would go off with ammunition and other supplies and return in the spring with their pelts."

Josèphe had a long memory and a ready tongue. Once started he entertained them all evening with stories of his youthful adventures. "On this north shore," he said, "there was always a race in the spring between us and the English traders from Albany to be first at the mouths of the rivers – the Credit, the Toronto and the Rouge. I have seen as many as a hundred English canoes heading across the lake to Oswego laden with the furs we had hoped to get – *our* furs from *our* Indians – Sapristi! Usually, though, we would arrive first with boatloads of trading goods and be waiting for the Ottawas and other western tribes when they came in over the Toronto Portage loaded down with pelts from as far west as Sault Ste. Marie and Michilimackinac.

"I remember when Fort Toronto was built in 1750 to protect the fur trade and I was there nine years later when it was abandoned. Word came that Quebec had fallen to the British and Captain Douville, acting on orders from the Governor, burned the fort and retired with his garrison to Montreal. Tomorrow, as we pass the spot I'll show you where it stood."

For days they paddled down Lake Ontario past an uninhabited shore where huge trees came down to the very water's edge. When the wind was from the west the men hoisted a sail and, shipping their paddles, promptly fell asleep. At such times they floated, a tiny human craft suspended between the limitless sky and a vast expanse of lake. Eventually they reached the portage at the Carrying Place where only a narrow neck of land separated

Lake Ontario from the sheltered waters of the Bay of Quinté.

Pastor Schmidt became quite excited. "From Quinté to Cataraqui," he said to Mary, "the Front is lined with Loyalist farms and many of the settlers are my friends – men of German descent who, like your uncle, fought for the crown in the King's Royal Regiment of New York."

That evening, while the pastor held a Lutheran service in the home of one of his friends, Mary called on the Indians at the Tyendinaga Reserve. She got no news, however, for Chief Deseronto and his Mohawk braves were all, like Brant, away at the big Indian conference.

In the morning they paddled on down the shore to Cataraqui. This turned out to be a town of about fifty log and frame houses clustered around a small stone tower on low land at the river's mouth. Mary was puzzled. "But where" she asked, "is Fort Frontenac?"

"It was destroyed years ago by the British. Only the ruined stone walls remain," replied the pastor, "Inside them you will find the new barracks where you must go to ask about your brother. The commanding officer speaks French so you should be able to manage alone while I attend to my business. We must both hurry because Pépin thinks it may snow soon and he wants to be well into the Thousand Islands by nightfall."

Mary made her way to the Barracks, bracing herself for the ordeal of questioning a strange officer. A soldier led her to an inner room where an officer resplendent in red and gold sat busily writing behind a desk piled with papers. He did not appear to notice her. "Monsieur," she said politely in French, "will you please help me?"

The Major looked up, surprised to see before him a white girl dressed like an Indian, fair enough to be English and yet speaking French. "What can I do for you?" he asked.

She quickly explained her errand and he told her he had never heard of such a boy as Johnny in the family of any of his officers. "But wait," he added, and he absentmindedly dipped his quill pen in and out of a stone ink jar on the desk. "It is just possible," he continued then, "that Miss Molly might be able to help you. I am speaking of Molly Brant. Do you know who I mean?"

Of couse she knew. Who did not know of the beautiful and brilliant Molly Brant, sister of Chief Joseph Brant of the Mohawks, who had married Sir William Johnson the British agent of Indian Affairs and had born him eight children.

"Does Miss Molly speak French?" queried Mary.

"Yes. She has been living in Montreal and on Carleton Island and now the Governor has built her a house in Cataraqui. Serjeant, show this young lady to Miss Molly's house," and the major turned back to his dispatches.

The serjeant led her through town to a large new house beside the river. She knocked and the door was opened by a negro woman who showed her into the drawing room and went to find her mistress. To Mary, who had never been inside any but the most primitive of pioneer homes, the furnishings were amazing; carpets, curtains and upholstered chairs, pewter candlesticks and brass fire irons. Attracted by blue and white china plates displayed on a dresser shelf, she had just crossed the room to have a closer look at them when she heard a sound behind her and turned to find a handsome woman framed in the doorway. The high cheek bones, black hair and flashing black eyes were unmistakably Mohawk but the woman was dressed in European style, in a flowered silk dress with a ruffle of lace around her neck.

"I am Molly Brant," she said. "Who are you?" Then before Mary could answer she continued rather sharply, "You are white. Why do you wear Indian clothes?"

"Because I *am* Indian," answered Mary holding her head high. Then, her blue eyes snapping, she continued, "I am an adopted daughter of the Delaware."

"I am glad to know you are proud of it," said Miss Molly in a gentler tone. "Now, sit down and tell me what I can do for an adopted daughter of the Delaware."

As briefly as she could Mary told the reason for her visit.

Miss Molly leaned forward impressively, "Did you know," she said, "that by a law passed two years ago in New York State all the tribes had to hand over their white captives to the authorities at either Albany or Fort Stanwix? I suggest you search among the whites in those towns for the two older boys. As for your sister Sarah, she must be about twenty-four and is probably married by now to a Seneca."

"I wondered about that myself," said Mary.

"In that case go to the Seneca sachems at Little Beardstown on the Genesee to enquire for her. Now about your little brother, the one you call Johnny, I'll see if I can locate him as I know most of the British officers. If I find him where will you be?"

"I'll be living with my uncle Jacob Sheets on the Long Sault. Thank you very much for helping me."

Miss Molly suddenly began to laugh. "Doesn't it

seem funny," she said, "that you who are white wear Indian clothes and I who am red dress like a white woman?"

"Not so strange. I think the Great Manitou loves us all the same no matter what we wear or whether our skin is white or red."

"I agree. Or even half and half," added Miss Molly, thinking of her children.

Mary thanked her again and left, hurrying back to the big canoe. She looked so happy and excited the men thought she must have found her brother. "No, not yet," she explained, "but I met the famous Molly Brant and she has promised to look for him."

A couple of nights later they were camping in a little cove on the north shore of the St. Lawrence when Pépin, who usually was very quiet, began to talk. "At one time," he said, "all this district on both sides of the river was called Oswegatchie. We French used to have a flourishing shipyard here and a five-star fort to protect it. Right here where we are sitting is Point au Baril where the British General Amherst in the summer of 1760 mustered his 10,000 redcoats and 700 Indians on his way from Cataraqui to attack Montreal. When our tiny French garrison here saw him coming they burned the fort and retired downstream to Fort Levis on Isle Royale. There they held out for two days against overwhelming numbers. That was the last battle in North America between the French and English because Montreal capitulated without a fight." He was silent for a moment, then added, "My father was killed in that battle."

Next morning as they paddled past Isle Royale, with the great ruined chimney of Fort Levis pointing skyward like a monument to the brave men who once defended it, Pépin nodded towards it, crossing himself as he did so.

"White water," announced Jean a short time later, rising to stand in the prow to guide them through the foaming waves of the Galops Rapids. Now Mary knew why the bowman and steersman had paddles twice as long as the others. Pépin in the stern was standing too, steering with his eight-foot paddle while the middlemen held their shorter ones poised for instant action. The speed now accelerated tremendously and dangerous looking rocks seemed to be rushing upstream to meet them. A few minutes later they floated out smoothly on a quieter section of the river.

"Rapid Plat next," said Jean, "and then the Long Sault."

"But we won't run the Long Sault," stated Pépin. "The North Channel is too dangerous unless we pick up a pilot."

Once they had passed the Rapid Plat, Pastor Schmidt began pointing out the homes of Lutheran settlers whom he knew. "There's John Crysler's farm," he said, "and Boucks – Weavers – Snyders – Loucks. There's Ault's Creek, Farran's Point and Fikes – "

Mary was not listening. A spasm of fear had suddenly gripped her. The journey was almost over and soon she would have to say goodbye to her friends of the fur brigade and prepare to meet unknown relatives. Would they like her? Would she like them? Why had she ever left the kind and comfortable farm home of the LeBlancs and come all this way to live with strangers?

A steady roaring sound announced the great rapids ahead and the current became swifter. They passed wooded islands on their right and clearings on the left, where a path showed between the bare branches of the trees with children on it, running. Evidently they had spotted the big canoe and were trying to reach the landing ahead of it. Striding along behind the children was a young man.

"Well, here we are at Hoople Creek," said Pastor Schmidt.

Hoople? the name sounded vaguely familiar. Then Mary remembered it was the surname of the boy who had once come with her cousin Bill to her home in Pennsylvania, his friend Henry with the laughing blue eyes.

"Yes," continued the pastor. "The Creek is named for the man who lives in that cabin."

Mary looked with interest at the cabin. That would be Henry's home she supposed and the woman in the doorway holding the baby was probably his wife. But there was no more time for surmising. They had docked and Jean was waiting to hand her out. The pastor was already on the wharf talking to the man who had come down with the children.

"This is your cousin, Bill Sheets," said the pastor.

Bill stepped forward, arms outstretched to welcome her. She thought he did look a little like the boy who had visited them long ago on Chillisquaque Creek, but older and distressingly thin.

She was shocked to see the children in an advanced stage of starvation, begging the voyageurs for food. Apparently the men had expected this for they had prepared a pile of sea biscuits to give to them – one to each child.

A tall Indian now strode down to the landing and began talking to Pépin while the rest of the crew relaxed with their pipes.

"Who is he?" asked Mary.

"That is the river pilot for the Long Sault," answered the pastor, "a Mohawk from St. Regis, Catholic and French speaking."

The pilot stepped into the canoe and prepared to direct it through the rapids. Pépin put Mary's chest on the wharf and said goodbye. She thanked him and the pastor and the agent for the good voyage; and then she went the rounds of all the men, shaking hands with each, and thanking them for the safe and happy trip.

As Pépin pushed off towards the raging waters of the Long Sault the voyageurs raised their paddles in a farewell salute and burst into song spontaneously, "Vive la Canadienne et ses jolis yeux doux."

Mary waved and watched as the canoe gained speed then twisted and turned in the mountainous waves. The pilot, standing in the prow, directed the paddlers with hand signals for they could not possibly have heard his voice above the noise of the rapids. Suddenly the boat turned completely around and disappeared from sight. Mary gasped. Minutes later it appeared again much farther away with all hands paddling – safe beyond the clutches of the greatest rapids in the St. Lawrence.

Bill then shouldered her wooden chest and led her westward up the River Road to her uncle's home.

Chapter 17

THE LONG SAULT

Bill chatted away cheerfully in German, not realizing that Mary had forgotten all she ever knew of that language and could not understand him. Taking her silence for shyness he continued to point out the sights as they passed them. On the left he indicated the heavily wooded islands of Long Sault, Diables and Trois Chenailles Ecartes the latter known locally as Sny Island, and beyond them across the border in New York State the distant blue peaks of the Adirondacks. On their right he showed her the new log homes of the settlers, each one standing proudly among blackened stumps in its clearing. "Cryderman's, Pratts, Philips, and Lieutenant Maun's," he said.

Mary's ears buzzed with the constant roar of the rapids, from the bush came the ring of busy axes, and over everything hung a haze of smoke from burning brush fires. For a distance the road became little more than a footpath through the thick bush of as yet uncleared lots, then it emerged once more into the open where little houses of peeled logs shone golden in the rays of the setting sun, their paleness accentuated by the dark wall of forest behind them. "McKenzie Morgan's," said Bill, "Serjeant Bill Mordan's, Dan Mordan's and – Sheets."

At the name "Sheets" Mary's attention was rivetted on the farthest house. Like the others along the Front it had only one small window and was built of round logs mortised to fit together at the corners. From the some- what primitive-looking chimney rose a comfortable curl of smoke and in the doorway, waiting to welcome her, stood her uncle and his wife, Catherine.

As they came closer she saw that her uncle Jacob looked very much like her mother. When he put his arms around her and hugged her tight she found a lump rising in her throat and surprised herself by stammering *"Mein Mutter* - My mother."

The German phrase came easily to her lips out of the past but it was the only one that did. Her newly found relatives talked steadily in German but she had no idea what they were saying. She stood there in distress, unable to respond, her mind filled with a mixture of French and Delaware words that were of no use at all. Like Bill, they put her silence down to shyness and led her into the house.

How much this cabin reminded her of her old home in Pennsylvania! - the same bunk beds against the walls, the same fieldstone and mud fireplace, the rough- hewn pine table and benches and the hooks and shelves here and there for clothes and supplies. With a little gasp of recognition she went straight to the German hymnal lying on its special shelf. Laying her hand on it she said, the syllables coming back to her slowly across the years, "Mar - burg - er Ges-un - buch."

They all nodded with pleasure and indicated that she was to join them at the supper table. Her uncle then asked her a direct question in German but she could only shake her head and say, *"Kein Deutsch* - No German."

They were shocked. It had never occurred to them that she might have forgotten her mother's tongue.

"Do you speak English?" asked Bill, hopefully.

Again she could only shake her head. But it took no language of any kind to eat. Her aunt placed steaming bowls of soup at each place and beside these a tiny cake. At the guest's place she put two of these little cakes and Mary recognised this as a sign of generous hospitality and an indication of real scarcity. Evidently the rumours about crop failure and starvation were all too true.

The soup tasted unmistakably of dried beech leaves and of nothing else. The cakes appeared to contain traces of oatmeal, cornmeal and wild rice mixed with a generous portion of sawdust. Her hosts were watching her anxiously so she took care to keep her face expressionless the way she had learned to do in the wigwams of the Delaware. She had no way of knowing until long afterwards that each of the ingredients in those cakes represented the sacrificial last scrapings of some neighbour's meal barrel given to help the Sheets welcome her into their midst.

There was no mistaking the signs of famine. She knew them well from personal experience on the Allegheny: the hollow cheeks and shrunken frames, the lacklustre eyes. Starvation was indeed stalking the land - but why? Why? Why? Why? she wondered with a limitless forest at their back door surely they could find something more sustaining to eat than beech leaf soup!

It was at this point that she remembered Madame LeBlanc's packages which Antoine Chauvin had brought to her on the dock at Detroit. She got up from the table and unlocked her chest. Giving the packages to her uncle she tried to make him understand by signs that these were a gift to him from her Detroit friends.

Bill and Catherine watched while he opened them, their excitement mounting as he unwrapped sea biscuits and pemmican. With shaking fingers Jacob put a biscuit at each place while his wife cut up some pemmican and set it to soften in water over the fire. Then they all sat down and had a second supper, the Sheets trying pitifully hard not to appear eager for the food.

After the wooden bowls were washed and dried Mary entertained the family by unpacking her chest. She had no idea that Madame's cast-off clothes would cause such a sensation. She had to shake them out for, although dry now, they were still crumpled after the soaking they got in the storm on Lake Ontario. As she displayed them she said, "Madame, Detroit," and pointed to herself.

Catherine was entranced. She was sick and tired of her own dress, her one and only grey linsey-woolsey made exactly like those of all the other loyalist women four years before from government yardage given out at Sorel. At that time they had been thankful for dresses to replace the tattered garments in which they had escaped through the wilderness from the wrath of the American revolutionaries, but by now they were tired of them. To Catherine Madame's long blue petticoat and short fawn overdress, with the white cap and apron to go with it, were like a fashion show from the outer world. She exclaimed over the little blue scarf that Mary used to tie over her hair and clucked with admiration as she fingered the softness of the crimson wool shawl which had been Madame's parting gift to Mary.

Mary was amused. She still liked her Indian doe-skins best and loved the elaborate quillwork which decorated them. They were comfortable and practical for camping and walking through bush trails and they were dear to her because Mother Medicine had made them for her. She was glad that Catherine did not seem to be going to make a fuss about their smell the way Madame had done.

The family then sat around the blazing log fire and the two men made it clear by signs that they wished to know all about the Whitmore massacre and the fate of the other children. She was surprised because she had thought they must already have heard about it, else how had they known enough to search for her? This was a puzzle and the answer to it would have to wait until she learned to speak German. Meantime she did the best she could by pantomime to demonstrate the scalping of her parents and Phillip and then she acted out the tragic fate of the baby. After that, saying "Sarah, Peter, George, Johnny, Mary," she tied Catherine's arms together behind her back and pretended to march her off captive.

They got the picture. Then she said, "Sarah, Peter, George - Senecas." They nodded. She added, "Johnny, Mary - Delawares." They got that too. But how to tell about the happy years in her Delaware home or how the British officer took Johnny away after four years or how and why she had bound herself out for a year to René LeBlanc in Detroit was beyond her powers of acting.

"Jake?" queried Bill, "Catherine? Ann?

So he remembered all their names! Mary wished she knew of their fate to tell him but she did not. She shrugged her shoulders and spread out her hands as if to say, "I don't know."

At bedtime Mary crawled into her bunk, wishing she could sleep under the stars as she had done on the trip east instead of indoors in a stuffy house. Long after the others had gone to sleep she lay there going over the events of the day and listening to the incessant roar of the rapids.

Visitors began arriving in the morning – neighbours, friends, relatives curious to meet the newcomer. They had all heard with horror of the Whitmore massacre. Some of them had known Mary's mother when she was a girl, and they had been thrilled when news came from Pastor Schmidt that he had found one of the children. They were now eager to meet her and to hear her story but like the Sheets they were disappointed that she could not understand them or speak to them in either German or English. All they could do was to smile their welcome and finger the quillwork on her doeskins in admiration. To entertain them she and Catherine passed around the sea biscuits.

As soon as she could Mary slipped away into the bush for a couple of hours and came back with a medium sized eel and a pile of Wapatoo or Indian Potatoes. The Sheets were delighted. They thought they had long ago eaten the last of the eels but to Mary's disappointment they refused to touch the Wapatoo. She fried these in eel oil and put a pile at each place but they shook their heads violently and pushed them away. She understood their fear of poisoning and that they really had no reason as yet to trust her knowledge of edible plants. By now she herself had developed quite an appetite. If they would not eat the Wapatoo she would, and did. They watched her anxiously, evidently expecting her to drop dead at any moment.

Catherine saved some of the eel for the Cook family, their next door neighbours to the west, and taking Mary with her she went to call on them. There they found a son of the house pacing the floor in agony from an earache. Mary's professional interest was roused and she left the house abruptly and went out into the bush to search for the cure.

It was difficult so late in November to find anything in the forest - too late to expect flowers or leaves or fruit on the plants by which to identify them - but Mary was not daunted. She asked the Great Manitou to direct her to a wild hop vine and then it seemed as if an unseen hand led her straight to one. She left that plant untouched, according to Delaware medicinal practice, and began searching for another. This, when she found it, had still a few hops dangling from a stem. She put them into a little skin bag and took it home to the Sheets house to heat it by the fire. Then she returned to the Cook home.

She entered as suddenly and silently as she had left, walked up to the boy and held the hot bag against his ear, indicating that he was to keep it there. Catherine and the Cooks were startled but seeing that this medicine was external only, they did not interfere. In a short time the lad showed signs of relief and the earache gradually disappeared.

Mary went home with Catherine and forgot all about the incident but the neighbours did not. They spread the story up and down the Front: "That Whitmore girl," they said, "Jacob Sheets' niece who was captured by the Indians, knows how to cure an earache and can find food in the bush."

Hope. A glimmer of hope came with this news to a desperate people living in hazardous pioneer conditions many miles from a doctor. Faced with crop failure and famine they grasped at this straw of hope, perhaps the Whitmore girl would turn out to be the answer to their prayers. But they were cautious - they watched and waited. Let others, they said, try her roots first before they risked poisoning themselves with them.

The next evening Mary was stirring the pemmican mixture over the fire when she happened to drop the wooden spoon and exclaimed inadvertently in French, *"Quel dommage, c'est sale maintenant* - What a pity it is dirty now."

Bill immediately replied in French without thinking, "*Ca ne vaut rien, ma petite* - Never mind Little One."

Mary straightened up, the spoon in her hand, her mouth open in surprise. "Bill! You speak French!"

"Why certainly," he answered in that language, "what else would you expect after three years in the army at Isle Aux Noix and Montreal?"

"How wonderful! Now we can really talk and I can ask you questions about all I have been longing to know and I won't have to struggle any more to find out what Uncle and Aunt are trying to tell me."

From then on Bill took her under his wing, explaining things to her in French and translating for her in the evenings while she described the harrowing details of the massacre and of her happy life with the Delaware. She was now able to tell them how Johnny had been taken away by the British officer and how she came to live with the LeBlancs in Detroit. It was like an exciting serial story, told bit by bit and relayed every day by Catherine to the neighbours who waited eagerly for each new instalment and passed it on in turn to all whom they met.

On Sunday the family attended the Lutheran Lay Service held in the Markle home a short distance down the River Road and Mary found herself seated between Catherine and Bill. Every once in a while he whispered to her in French, telling her who was who in the crowded room. "That little man up front with the flute is John Hoople," he said, "a brother of my friend Henry who went with me to visit you in Pennsylvania."

"Is Henry here too?" she asked.

"No. He lives here but he is away hunting just now."

Mary's attention was then caught by the music for the man with the flute was playing a tune that was familiar to her, the very hymn tune that she remembered best from the family services of her childhood, *"Ein feste Burg - A Safe Stronghold Our God Is Still."*

On the way home from church she told Bill about her problem, explaining that she feared to teach the Long Sault settlers how to find food in the forest when she could not speak their language in case they misunderstood her instructions and poisoned themselves.

"Oh I can solve that easily," he replied. "I have no time to go with you myself but I'll bring the LaRace twins over to meet you. They talk both French and German. You instruct them in French and they in turn will tell the others in German."

Chapter 18

FOOD FROM THE FOREST

True to his word Bill came home a few days later accompanied by two slim dark youngsters of about fourteen years of age. "Celeste and Pierre LaRace," said he, introducing them. "This is my cousin Mary Whitmore who speaks only French and Delaware."

The twins grinned and nodded.

"She wants," he continued, "to show you some of the fancy tricks the Indians have for finding food in the bush. Then you can pass on the knowledge to the people in German."

"Bon!" exclaimed Pierre and Celeste in unison. "*Allons!* – Let's go." The three of them set out in high spirits, chatting in French all the way.

Mary decided that she had better train them thoroughly about one thing at a time, the way Little Doe and Mother Medicine had trained her long ago on the Allegheny. Forest potatoes was the first item on her market list so she led them deep into the forest to a spot where, as she already knew, the miniature vegetables were to be found. Then she explained carefully how to locate such a spot in winter when no leaves or flowers were in sight to guide them. "Search for a sunny open slope like this, facing south."

Mary scraped away the snow over a space of several square feet and then with the twins' help made small fires on the bare frozen earth to thaw it out. With a sharpened stick she prodded an inch or two below the surface for the little tubers.

Soon they had a pile of the tiny bulbs; some of them as small as the tip of Mary's finger, others about twice that size. They were small but food all the same – precious food for a starving population.

They lost no time in roasting these in the fires. Celeste and Pierre were as hungry as everyone else in the settlement and they ate ravenously, sitting on a fallen tree trunk in the companionable silence of the winter woods.

The twins were eager pupils and quick to learn but they did not locate the likely places with the certainty that Mary did. She knew exactly where to dig but she had not managed to impart to them just how she knew this. The twins would find a likely spot and point to it but Mary would say, "No." Another time they would indicate an almost identical place and she would say, "Yes" and sure enough she would be right.

She began to realize now that she had been using some inner knowledge that the twins did not have. It was her silent prayers to Manitou that made the difference but how was she to impart this important ritual to Celeste and Pierre? They might laugh at her Indian beliefs, beliefs that were so vital to her that she thought she could not bear to have them ridiculed. However, the lives of the starving people on the Long Sault were at stake and she must be brave enough to risk the ridicule.

Pierre gave her an opening. "How do you always find the right places and we do not?"

"Probably because I ask the Great Manitou for help. I say to him, 'Mighty One my people starve. Please show me where to find the food they need.' Then I go to the first likely spot and that is it."

"Oh, I know," said Celeste, "that's the way it worked when Moses asked God for water in the desert. He showed him where to strike the rock and water gushed out."

"Yes, Manitou is the Indian name for God."

To Mary's relief there was no ridicule and from then on the twins located forest potatoes nearly as often as she did.

Flour was the next item on Mary's market list so when they set out the following morning she said, "We must find a flour substitute today. It is time we had some kind of bread to eat with that everlasting soup."

"Flour!" scoffed Celeste, "You're crazy. Not a kernel is left from last summer's miserable crops – no corn, no wheat, no oats and all the wild rice has been found and eaten long since. So how can you make flour?"

"Come along with me and see. I have done it many times in my Indian home."

This time she led them to the swampy shore of Hoople Creek where it emptied into the St. Lawrence because there were cattails there in abundance. For this excursion she wore her buckskin leggings and brought with her the family hoe and three wooden buckets filled with spagnum moss.

She built a fire on shore and then, smashing a hole in the ice, filled the buckets with water. This done she plunged knee deep into the icy creek and with the hoe dug out piles of cattail roots.

"Come and help me wash them."

The twins, overcome with admiration at such fortitude, quickly responded, washing the mud and slime from the frozen roots. Then they gathered around the fire to get warm again, while Mary rubbed her legs with the spagnum moss to bring back the circulation.

They then cut the messy rope-like roots into short lengths, peeled the outer husks off them and washed the white inner core three times in cold water rubbing hard to get rid of the fibres. Finally when they had a deposit of wet white starch in the bottom of each pail, Mary said, "That is our flour. Now let us go home before I catch my death of cold. While we are warming ourselves we can make cattail cakes for supper and, of course, you two must stay and help to eat them."

The Sheets family was intrigued by this experiment but they had little faith in its success. Nevertheless they stayed close by, ready to eat the cakes if by any chance they really materialized.

The white starchy substance in the pails was still wet but Mary explained, the twins translating for her, that the wetness did not matter. She added a little salt, mixed in a few drops of eel oil and dropped the stuff by the spoonful onto a hot spider on the fire. She then put the lid on it and heaped hot coals on top of that.

By the time Mary's teeth had stopped chattering a delicious odour of baking drop cakes filled the house.

"It is a long time since I smelled anything so good," said Jacob Sheets in German; and Mary, understanding the gist of what he said, looked up in time to see tears in her uncle's eyes.

"We need some meat," said Mary as the three of them set out a few days later. Today we go turtle hunting.

Pierre threw back his head and laughed.

"Why do you laugh?"

Because our men long ago found and ate all the turtles in the countryside. I wager there is not one left between here and Montreal."

"Our people are woodsmen, you know, as well as farmers," added Celeste. "The LaRace family has been in Canada for over a hundred years. Naturally they know how to hunt. Even your German cousins have been in America long enough to understand the skill of turtle hunting."

For a second Mary was taken aback. Perhaps they were right. No doubt the settlers did know the turtle's habit of burying itself in mud for the winter months along the shores of creeks and rivers. But, on the other hand, maybe they did not know everything. They could not know as much as the Delaware did with their long race memory of famines in the past. Did they, for instance, know that in times of scarcity the wily old turtles avoided exposed places like the banks of creeks and buried themselves on islands instead? She doubted it.

Her Delaware training now stood her in good stead, for none of this uncertainty showed on her expressionless face. "Follow me," she said firmly.

They went inland several miles, blazing trees for their return route, until they reached a tributary of the Raisin River flowing eastward. They followed this downstream a way until Mary spotted an island sticking up above the surface ice of the creek. She built small fires all around its shore while Pierre and Celeste looked on with thinly veiled amusement, not bothering to help her.

When the ground had thawed sufficiently she began prodding it with a heavy pointed stick – apparently in vain. She had encircled the little island before her stick hit a turtle shell with a loud "klunk".

Pierre's indifference vanished, and he lunged towards the spot, his hatchet raised to strike.

"Mais Non," stormed Mary. "Don't touch it. This one we leave. The next one we take. Always we must spare the first one we find or the turtle will take revenge."

She carefully covered the creature again with earth and snow and moved on to find another island. Pierre and Celeste followed her sulking.

On the next island they hit turtles almost at once and this time killed three big ones, but not before Mary had apologized to each of them in Delaware translating her words for the benefit of the twins. "I am sorry Brother Turtle to have to do this to you but our people are starving and they must have food."

"But," protested Celeste, "I do not believe that trees and animals have spirits so why should I apologize to them or spare them?"

Mary shrugged. "The Great Manitou made the trees and the animals as well as people and he put a piece of his own spirit in each. Besides, if you kill all the turtles this year there will be none at all next year. An Indian always spares the first game that he finds."

"But we are not Indians," objected Pierre.

"That is true. No Indian would need to starve in this forest of plenty the way your people have been doing."

"Touché," said Pierre. "You win."

Chapter 19

DOCTOR GIRL

"I came for – the doctor girl," the terrified boy in the doorway, exhausted by his cross-country run, gasped for breath between words, his eyes wide with fright. "My mother – I think – she is –", he choked over the last word, "dying."

He spoke in German but Mary now knew a few words of that language and grasped his meaning. She and Catherine exchanged glances. An interpreter was needed but Bill was away in New Johnstown with a load of potash, hoping to exchange it there for a few supplies.

"Celeste." That was the solution. They said her name simultaneously and Mary went immediately to find her while Catherine gave the boy some hot soup to revive him.

Celeste came willingly and translated the details, so that Mary knew the nature of the disease she was to doctor and could take with her the necessary medicines. The Boy's name was Otto Kine. His mother had been ill with diarrhea for some time and was growing weak. His father was away in Montreal, the younger children hungry and crying. The neighbours were trying to help but the only cure they knew was boiled milk and there was no milk. In fact there was not a single cow on the whole of the Long Sault in 1787.

"Please, doctor girl, come," he pleaded.

Mary and Celeste went with him to his home several miles inland, stopping en route to locate the wild cherry trees that Mary had previously noticed and to strip them of bark. The best Delaware cure for diarrhea was wild cherry bark pounded into pulp and boiled in water.

When they reached the cabin they found Mrs. Kine in a serious condition, weakened by both hunger and disease. Neighbours agreed to take the younger children temporarily into their homes while Mary doctored the sick woman, and Celeste took Otto out into the bush in search of food.

In a week the woman had recovered and gained some strength from the food they found for her – wild honey, forest potatoes, a few eels. Then Mary and Celeste were able to leave for home.

The story of Mrs. Kine's cure travelled out to the Front ahead of them and Mary now found herself in constant demand to doctor fevers, toothaches, ague, arthritis and other ailments. She was kept busy searching for herbs and roots as well as for food, and this became very difficult as the cold grew more intense, the ground harder and the snow deeper.

One day, alone in the forest and a long way from home, Mary set a fire burning to thaw out the ground where she expected to dig for roots. She used the waiting period to break ice on a nearby creek, scoop up a goodly supply of Wapatoo tubers with her bare toes and set some of these to bake in the ashes of the fire. She was briskly rubbing her feet with spagnum moss after this chilly occupation when her sharp Indian-trained eye caught a movement in the distance between the bare tree trunks – a man was approaching on snowshoes, carrying a musket and a pair of Jack rabbits and stumbling slightly as though he were weak from hunger.

"But why hunger?" she asked herself, her quick brain dealing with the situation almost before she was aware of it. If he had two rabbits, why not eat them? As the man came closer she saw he was of medium height and heavily bearded. He greeted her in German but she shook her head.

"Je ne parle que français," she said.

"Fine, I speak French too." He sat down on a fallen tree, placed the rabbits on the ground beside him and began warming his hands over the fire. "I smelled your smoke way back and came to see what you were cooking."

"Wapatoo," said Mary, "Indian potatoes. Would you like some?" She pulled a few well-baked specimens out of the ashes with a forked stick and offered them to him. There was no mistaking the eager way he reached for them – ate them, and yet the rabbits lay untouched beside him! She began munching wapatoo herself sitting down companionably on a nearby log.

"Those are unusual snowshoes you have there," he remarked between bites.

"They are made in the Delaware style," she answered.

"Oh, you have Delaware connections,"

"I lived with them on the Allegheny for seven years."

"No wonder you know how to find Indian potatoes. And where do you live now?"

"With relatives on the Front on the Long Sault. I have just come here from Detroit."

"Tell me about Detroit. How big is it?" He was speaking in an absent-minded way while eagerly watching every move she made, evidently hoping she would pull more potatoes from the fire. To oblige him she did.

She liked his deep quiet voice and there was something vaguely familiar about his dark blue friendly eyes as he looked at her in a way that made her feel she could trust him.

She described Detroit to him while he ate. "There are several hundred houses, some stores and a church with bells, and two forts all surrounded by a stockaded wall with bastions at each corner. Out in front on the river are several wharves with vessels of all sizes. I lived outside the walls on a river farm where it is very beautiful. The farmhouses are surrounded by orchards and in the spring there are clouds of pink and white blossoms, with the blue river in front with white sails of the ships, and big windmills turning in the wind." She found herself feeling homesick for her old life with the LeBlancs.

He nodded. "Before the Revolutionary War," he said, "I had a farm in the Colony of New York and in the spring you wouldn't believe how beautiful it was. There were wild cherry blossoms all down the valley in front of our house. It was a good house," he added dreamily, "I helped my father build it, and we had a good farm. I worked it with him until he died and then by myself afterwards. I loved that farm and then because we lost the war they confiscated it. My life's work gone for nothing!"

She caught the depth of bitterness in his voice. "You are young," she said. "Can't you build another one here?"

He looked at her keenly, "Yes, I can. That's what I aim to do but do you know the work it takes, the backbreaking never-ending work, to clear the land beginning from scratch with nothing to work with but your strength and your own two hands and an axe?"

"And courage perhaps?"

"You question the courage of a man who fought through the war in the King's forces?" He stopped eating. "I think I know what you mean, though. A man needs a special kind of courage to pioneer and can only succeed if he has it."

"Yes, I think so. My father had it."

"Tell me more about yourself. Who are the relatives you are living with on the Front?"

"The Sheets, Jacob Sheets."

"I thought so. I was just beginning to put two and two together. From what you say you must be one of his nieces, one of the Whitmore girls from Shamokin in Pennsylvania. I visited them once in '79 before the family was massacred. You must be one of those who escaped. Which one? No. Wait. Don't tell me. See if I can guess." He leaned forward and examined her features intently. "I know," he said, "You are the youngest girl, Polly."

Her face lit up with pleasure at the use of her childhood nickname. "You must be Bill's friend Henry." she said.

"That's right. You had long, tawny-coloured pigtails and gave me a birchbark picture you had drawn. Remember?"

"Yes, I remember, and you went with me to the spring for water and carried the bucket for me." At that moment her eyes fell on the Jack rabbits and suddenly she thought she knew why he had not eaten them himself – he was taking them home to his wife.

He helped her to dig up the roots she needed and extinguish the fire and then they followed the trail out to the Front together chatting easily as they went.

"I leave you here," said Mary, when they reached the fork in the trail where one path led downward to the Creek, and the other upriver towards the Sheets cabin. She went home to mix potions and attend to her patients.

That evening as she sat making a pair of snowshoes for Catherine she looked deep into the glowing hardwood coals and sighed. Henry seemed so much nicer than anyone else she had ever met, steadier, kinder, more friendly and he had some other quality that she could not quite pinpoint. One which made her feel as if she had known him well all her life.

Chapter 20

THE STORM

Mary was constantly called to doctor people and she was glad because it left little time to think of the pleasant companion who had eaten wapatoo with her in the bush. Her two most challenging patients were an old lady called Granny Rickert, crippled with rheumatism and a young man named Adam Weisner suffering from a festering bullet wound.

Weisner had accidentally tripped over his own gun while out hunting and shot himself in the thigh. The wound had been neglected so long Mary almost despaired of saving his life. She removed the buried bullet with a sharp knife, cleansed out the wound with a concoction of white elm bark and bound it up with a poultice of white oak as she had often seen Mother Medicine do in similar cases. But no matter what she gave him for his fever – boneset, healall, horsemint, it showed no improvement.

Granny Rickert appeared to grow worse daily instead of better under Mary's devoted care. Something drastic had to be done for her – but what? The only remedy Mary had not yet tried was the sweat house cure. Could she make a sweat house, she wondered, and persuade the old lady to crawl into it? She decided to try.

First she collected all the necessary supplies,

twelve of everything because that was the traditional number required for a Delaware sweat house. She gathered twelve flexible saplings, each about eight feet long, twelve hardwood logs for the fire to be built inside the hut, twelve rocks to be heated in the fire and a pile of skins and bark with which to roof the finished lodge. When all was ready she set twelve fires burning in a circle at evenly spaced points where she planned to drive in the poles. Once the ground thawed sufficiently she began to push and twist the poles into the earth. It was hard work. She was struggling with the third pole when she heard behind her a familiar voice.

"What are you doing? Let me help you."

She turned to see Henry standing there, clean shaven now, and looking both younger and thinner without his beard. She was annoyed with herself the way her spirits rose at the sight of him, and as a result she spoke more sharply than she knew.

"Oh no, thanks. Bill will give me a hand when he comes home."

"Very well."

The hurt puzzled look on his face as he walked away smote her. She struggled on alone with the poles.

After a while Henry came back accompanied by Bill and the two men set to work but Henry ignored her altogether, addressing all his remarks to Bill. Soon the twelve saplings were in position and she showed them how to overlap them on top, tying them together with vines to make a dome-shaped hut which they then covered with skins, setting the logs and stones inside in the centre ready for action.

Much to Mary's surprise Bill then invited Henry to stay for supper. This was a custom that had been abandoned in the settlement since the famine, for each family had all it could do to feed its own members. She was glad that the results of her last foraging trip made it possible for Bill to extend this hospitality. She went in to help prepare the meal and she was so quiet and preoccupied that Catherine glanced enquiringly at her several times.

Half way through supper Bill looked across the table at Henry and said, "Isn't it about time John built a house of his own for him and Elinor?"

"I suppose so but he doesn't seem keen on the idea and I hate to deliberately put them out."

Mary wondered if she had heard correctly. If Elinor was to move out with John then she must be John's wife and not Henry's. She was surprised at the joy that sprang up in her heart.

"Some day," Henry was speaking to Bill but looking directly at Mary and holding her eyes with his, "I'll want a wife of my own and then I guess I'll have to ask John to move."

Flustered Mary dropped her eyes to her bowl. Could he mean her?

For several weeks after that she saw nothing of Henry. She was busy giving Granny Rickert a series of steam baths in the sweat house and she had to be very firm with herself in order to keep her mind on the patient instead of day-dreaming about a possible future with Henry Hoople. She overcame the old lady's objections by taking the treatment with her, leaving the twins outside each time to close the opening and to hand in supplies when they were needed.

Inside the hut, when the fire had burned down to ashes and the rocks were hot, Mary administered a dose of herbal tea to make her patient perspire and then poured buckets of water over the hot stones to produce steam while she prayed earnestly to the Great Manitou to relieve the old lady of her pain and stiffness.

When the last treatment took place the neighbours gathered outside with the twins, curious to see how the experiment had worked. None of them really expected a cure. When the old lady crawled out of the entrance hole and stood upright, swinging her arms and declaring herself free of pain, they were astonished. The more pessimistic among them predicted that this would not last long, but they were wrong. Granny Rickert walked to church the following Sunday for the first time in years and her cure was the sensation of the week.

After that others wanted to try the steam bath but Mary refused. She was so busy doctoring Adam Weisner that she had no time to bother with any except the seriously ill.

Adam grew daily worse and Mary was forced to conclude that her incantations were inadequate because her whole heart and mind was not in them. She remembered Mother Medicine's solemn warning, "A Delaware shaman who means business must put all thoughts of his personal affairs right out of his mind and lay himself out in humbleness before the Great Spirit."

There were only two more treatments for fever that Mary knew of which she had not yet tried on Adam. One was made from hepatica leaves, the other from the root of ginseng, both of them difficult to find in the dead of winter. She hoped that a determined search for them, coupled with whole-hearted concentration, might succeed where all else had failed and with this in mind she went one day into the forest.

She had just located some hepatica leaves under the snow and was in the middle of performing the propitiatory rites when Henry came towards her through the trees. She was so glad to see him she stopped in the middle of an incantation.

"What have you there?" he asked.

"Hepatica leaves. I am preparing a strong medicine with them for Adam Weisner's fever."

"Lucky man."

"No. He is not lucky at all. He will die soon if I don't find a cure for him." She sighed as she spoke and looked distressed, remembering that she had come out on purpose to give her whole attention to Adam's recovery and here she was growing excited instead at the sight of Henry.

"Do I also have to shoot myself to gain your attention?" he asked.

She felt his gaze on her and looked up to see his eyes full of laughter. His look brought colour to her cheeks, a sparkle to her eyes and made the corners of her mouth turn upward in an irrepressible smile.

They chatted comfortably about their families and experiences, their likes and dislikes and their hopes. She told him about her search for Johnny and he described his little brother Franz, whom he and John had been obliged to leave behind them with revolutionary relatives in New York. Mary found it as easy to talk to this man as it was to breathe.

"You know," said Henry, looking serious, "I've been thinking of what you said about courage and I believe you are right. It does take a special kind of courage to persevere in building a homestead farm. Left to myself I don't have it. At Cherry Valley it was my mother who gave it to me. When I was blue or discouraged she cheered me up, when I was bored she gave me vision and always she inspired me to do my best."

"Where is your mother now?"

"She died during the war. What I'm trying to say to you, Polly is," and his eyes grew dark with intensity while his voice became husky, "what I am trying to say is – will you marry me and be my inspiration?"

She caught her breath, "Oh Henry, I'd love to." Then an expression of pain crossed her face. "Only – "

"Only what?"

"Only I have to care for Adam first." She had just remembered her duty as a shaman. "When he is cured I will. Please wait until he is better and then ask me again."

"Very well." Henry rose soberly and stood looking down at her. "I'll leave you now to finish making that medicine. I hope it is a strong potion that will cure him quickly." So saying he walked off through the trees.

Adam's condition did not improve. Now the ginseng cure was the only one left to try. Mary had seen some growing the day she and the twins went inland in search of turtles. She had memorized, at the time, a few landmarks to help her find the spot again if necessary and she expected the trail blazes they had left that day would still be discernable to guide her to the place.

The weather was bad, bitterly cold with high winds and drifting snow and she waited all day hoping it would clear. She felt terribly cooped up in the little cabin. She longed for fresh air and action and finally she could stand it no longer. She told Catherine she was going into the bush to hunt for ginseng.

Catherine was used to Mary's independent ways and knew she could take care of herself in the forest. So she only shrugged and went on patching Jacob's old army coat.

Mary soon located the blaze that showed where she and the twins had left the main trail, and she added a fresh cut to help her on the return trip. Then she moved along with confidence. At first she enjoyed pitting her strength against the elements but after a while she tired, for it was slow going through the drifts and fallen branches caused by the storm. Now and then she heard the thud of crashing trees and it began to dawn on her that she had been foolish to come out in such a blizzard. By this time, however, she had gone so far it seemed a pity to turn back without the ginseng and she kept on.

A sudden loud report stopped her as a giant pine ahead cracked at the base and began falling through the other trees with a wrenching sound. She hastily stepped backwards to avoid being struck and as she did so her right snowshoe caught in a root and threw her just as the pine crashed pinning her to the ground beneath its outer branches. Severe pain came from her right ankle where the snowshoe was twisted into a strange position and held there by the root as if in a vice. Her hatchet had flown out of her hand at the moment of impact and there was no way she could free herself from the branches. She was helpless.

Inaction in such bitter cold could lead only to freezing but she was powerless to move. To add to her troubles she now heard in the distance a sound that struck terror to her heart – the howling of wolves. The memory of her mother's voice came back to her across the years, "If you are ever alone – or in trouble remember that God loves you. Trust Him and ask for help. It will come."

Meantime in the Sheets' cabin Catherine was worried as the storm grew worse, not only for Mary but for her two men as well. Suddenly the door flew open and Henry appeared, covered with snow. "Where is Mary?" he asked.

"In the bush."

"In this storm? I had a feeling she was in danger and I came to see. I'm going after her. Where are Jacob and Bill?"

"At a meeting at Empey's."

"When they come home tell them where I've gone. I may need their help," and he went out into the blizzard slamming the door behind him.

The short January day was closing in, adding to the difficulty of seeing in the already gloomy woods. But once Henry had found the fresh blaze that showed where Mary had left the main trail he was able to follow her route from tree to tree. Like her he found it slow going for his way was littered with debris.

All at once there were no more blazes. He retraced his steps to the last mark and searched carefully in every direction without success. Bewildered he stood still and listened. Above the whistling of the wind he heard the howl of a wolf pack that has smelled its prey and is preparing to close in on it. His blood froze. Where was Mary? He called her. No answer. He fired his musket skyward to ward off the wolves and to let her know, if she were near, that help was at hand. Then he listened again.

There was a low moaning somewhere ahead of him. He saw the newly fallen tree and sick with fear in case he would find her crushed beneath it began to search. Something stirred.

"Polly, Polly, thank God you are alive!" He brushed off the snow which covered her and saw that she was pinned to the ground. "Are you hurt?"

"Just my ankle – broken I think. I can't move."

"Don't try. I'll cut away the limbs that hold you down."

He hacked off one branch after another until he was able to free her, removing her snowshoes and carefully examining the bad ankle.

"Sprained," he said, "no broken bones."

When he tried to sling her over his shoulders to carry her home she fainted and he was obliged to tie her wrists together around his neck and hold her by the knees around his waist with one hand, keeping the other for his musket, before he began the painful trip home from blaze to blaze.

The wolves were keeping their distance, wary of the gun. He had taken time to reload ready for an emergency but how long he could hold them at bay while he struggled through the drifts he did not know.

Crack came the unmistakable sound of a musket shot way ahead telling him that a search party must be coming. He fired his own in answer, reloaded and fired again – two shots to let them know he had heard their signal. Then he struggled on painfully, stumbling as he went under the heavy weight. Eventually he heard men's voices recognizing some as they came nearer, Bill's, Jacob's, Dan Mordon's. He made one more effort and fell exhausted as they came up through the trees, Mary, still unconscious, slid off his shoulders into their waiting arms.

When Henry came to he found himself stretched out on the floor before the fire in the Sheets home, with Bill beside him trying to force elderberry wine between his lips.

"Mary?" he asked anxiously.

"She is bad," said Bill, "She is over there in her bunk but dreadfully weak from so much exposure, barely conscious."

Henry got up and went over to the bunk. Her eyelids were closed, her breathing shallow. He leaned over.

"Polly," he urged, "look at me."

Her eyelids opened a fraction and closed again.

"Polly, come back," he said, his voice husky, "Come back. I need you."

Again her eyelids fluttered. This time they opened wide and a tiny smile flickered for a second at the corners of her mouth as her lips moved.

Henry leaned closer to catch the whispered words.

"I think – I need – you too."

Bowl used by Mary Whitmore Hoople to carry balm of gilead salve to her patients. Now in the Three Counties Museum at Cornwall, Ontario.

Chapter 21

THE REUNION

Mary and Henry were married and lived for the rest of their lives within sound of the Long Sault. They had twelve children eleven of whom grew up and prospered. Mary's services continued to be in demand as even two qualified doctors could not cope with the needs of the growing community and for many years she rode out on horseback to her patients carrying healing salves in her saddle-bags. Henry died in 1838 in his seventies but Mary, surrounded by children and grandchildren, lived on to the great age of ninety-one.

Meantime in 1851 Mary's lifelong dream of finding her brother Johnny came true. Her son William, a prosperous New York merchant, was in Toronto on business when he happened to overhear two men speaking of someone in Niagara named John Whitmore. Instantly alerted by the name he joined them and made enquiries. He learned that the man in question had been captured by Delaware Indians, had been rescued by a Captain Daniel Servos of the British Army, was adopted by him, brought up in the Servos family and had eventually married the Captain's daughter, Magdalene.

William went to Niagara-on-the-Lake to visit this John Whitmore and found out that he was indeed his mother's brother. He arranged for him to go by boat to the Long Sault to meet her. Then he wrote ahead to his mother to tell her the exciting news and prepare her for her brother's arrival.

The news of this dramatic event spread up and down "The Front" and inland even to the back concessions for Mary was known and respected for miles around and the story of the massacre of her parents and her own captivity had been told and retold in all the farm kitchens of the district. Consequently on the day of the event a great crowd gathered on the dock at Dickinson's Landing to await the arrival of the steamship from Prescott. Not only the Hooples and the Sheets but all their friends and neighbours and many more were there, some having thought up convenient errands at the Landing in order to be present at the reunion of the brother and sister.

Mary in a new dress sat with quiet dignity in the gig beside her eldest son, Gerry, and looked out over the green on Sheek's Island to the distant blue peaks of the Adirondaks.

As the steamer was sighted rounding a bend upriver Gerry handed his mother down from the carriage and they took their stand near the centre of the wharf in readiness for the great moment. For a while the sound of the approaching steamship was drowned out by the roar of the rapids, then they heard the scraping and bumping as it was made fast to the dock and the gangway set in place. Finally the passengers began to alight; a man and wife with four children, a couple of priests on their way to Quebec, several young businessmen full of self-importance and then a gap into which walked a stately old gentleman with white hair accompanied by a younger man. A sigh of anticipation rose from the waiting crowd as Mary on Gerry's arm moved forward – and then there they were – the two old people together again after seventy years, holding each other at arm's length and exclaiming over and over, "Mary-John", "John-Mary".

Mary's sons and daughters crowded around to meet their uncle and their children pressed in close behind them while the cousins and neighbours lingered on the outskirts enjoying every moment of the dramatic episode. Then John Whitmore was hustled into the gig and Gerry whipped up the horse with a fine flourish. The crowd made way for them and for the family procession of carts and buggies that followed as they moved off at a good clip towards the home of Jacob Sheets, the hundred-year old uncle of the Whitmores.

Mr. Sheets, almost totally blind, wept with joy when his nephew was brought to him and held out his hands to feel the face of his sister's son. He had specially requested that the first part of the visit should take place in his home and soon they were all seated in his comfortable living room prepared to relive the episodes of the massacre and catch up on family news of the intervening years.

John Whitmore had been only four when his parents were killed and naturally he had forgotten all but the bare outline of the event. He was anxious to hear from Mary, who had been about eleven at the time, the details that were missing in his own mind. William Kirby too, his son-in-law, who had accompanied him, being an historian and an author, was keen to hear her version of the massacre.

Jacob Sheets and the others present were more interested in finding out what new information John could contribute. As soon as Mary had finished Jacob addressed himself to John: "Now, nephew, tell us about yourself and your family."

"Well, sir, my wife Magadalene, as you may know, was the daughter of my benefactor, Captain Servos, and he gave us a farm at Niagara next to his own. We have two daughters: Ann, who is single and Eliza Magdalen who is married to this gentleman here beside you. Our three sons: Daniel, George and Peter, are all married and doing well with families of their own."

"Good, good. And do I understand that you are in the army?"

"Not the regular army, sir, I am in the militia, a captain in the 1st Lincoln Regiment. We were active at the siege of Fort Niagara in the War of 1812 and during the Rebellion of 1837."

"Well done. I was in the King's Royal Regiment of New York myself, served seven years under Sir John Johnson, in the Grenadier Company. That was the colonel's own company you know. We Sheets did our part too in the War of 1812, serving in the Stormont Militia. As to the Rebellion they wouldn't let me enlist for that. Said I was too old. Such nonsense I was only in my eighties and knew more about fighting than they did. Tell me how did this Captain Servos know where to find you?"

"One of Brant's Mohawks told him that he had seen a captive white boy with a band of Delawares on the Allegheny. I'll never forget the day he rode into our camp. I was terrified when I discovered he wanted to take me away because I loved my Indian family, especially my Indian mother."

"But I thought they tortured you, putting burning coals on your arms."

"Oh, yes, but that wasn't torture. That was a test to see if I was brave enough to be adopted into the tribe and" – here John drew himself up proudly, "and I was! Look here." He took off his coat, rolled up his shirt sleeves and showed them the scars on his inner arms.

Realizing that his uncle could not see, John put the old man's hand on his arm so that he could feel the scars.

John then took a small purse, beautifully embroidered in beadwork from his pocket and handed it to Mr. Sheets to feel. "My Indian mother gave me this," he said, "and I treasure it because I loved her."

"I loved my Indian mother too," said Mary "but it was cruel the way they separated the prisoners. All my life I've wanted to know what happened to you and the others and Sarah. Now I know about you which makes me feel better."

"And Sarah?" questioned John quickly. "Do you mean you don't know what happened to her?"

"No, I don't. If you do, tell me quickly. How is she? Where is she? I mean is she – is she alive?"

"No, my dear, not alive now. She died a long time ago. Two of her sons heard that I was in Niagara and came to see me. That is how I found out about her, wait a minute, I'd better begin at the beginning." With that John Whitmore settled himself more comfortably in his chair, crossed one leg over the other and paused for effect as many a storyteller will do once he is assured of an attentive audience.

Warming to his subject he began, "As you remember Sarah was the first to be separated from the rest of us. This was because she had been assigned to the Senecas who had to branch off early to the north to reach their home district on the Genesee River. They took her to their tribal village, Little Beardstown. While there she met and married another white captive named Horatio Jones. Later, after they had been freed from captivity by the Indian Treaty of 1785, he took her, so it is said to Schenectady where they were married in a Christian

176

service by the Reverend Samuel Kirkland.

"Horatio ran a fur trading station in the Finger Lakes Region for some years and then he moved his family back to the Genesee River to be with their friends the Senecas. By this time Horatio had become quite an important person since George Washington had appointed him American Interpreter to the Indians. He and Sarah had four sons, William, George, Hiram and James. It was George and James who came to see me. They said their mother had died the year after James was born and that their father had married again.

"The boys came to visit me several times but the last time was almost fatal. It was during the War of 1812 and these two lads, both officers in the United States Army stationed on the Niagara frontier, thought it would be a lark to borrow a boat, cross the Niagara River and visit their uncle inside the enemy lines on the Canadian shore. I was really horrified when they arrived for I knew that if they were seen inside British lines they might be taken for spies and shot on sight. Well, to cut a long story short, I hid them in my house while I went and explained the situation to my Colonel, who, because he knew and trusted me, sent the two lads back across the river unharmed except for a sound scolding."

Here John Whitmore paused as if he had difficulty in finishing the story, then he cleared his throat and continued in a subdued voice. "About two weeks later, when I was congratulating myself that the lads were safe, word came that both of them had been killed in the battle of Lewiston."

There was silence for a few minutes in the room, then Mary asked "What of Sarah's other sons?"

"They continued to live in Geneseo and I believe they were both married. I have been told that our brother

George had also settled there. That's all I know. Do you know what happened to our other brothers and sisters?"

"No, nothing except that my son William found out that Peter had been adopted by a farmer on the Mohawk River, grew up there and married and had a big family. William is going to try to visit them."

"And what about the ones in the sugar bush: Jake and Catherine and Ann?"

"I don't know anything about the girls but we did hear a vague rumour that reached us through a traveller from Pennsylvania that the boy, which would be Jake, had returned to the smoking ruins of his home and horrified at what he found had run all the way to Fort Augusta at Shamokin to get help and that the Rangers from there had gone out the next day and buried the dead."

Noticing that her Uncle Jake was looking exhausted from all the excitement Mary decided it was time for them to go. She rose, thanked him for his hospitality and said, "My daughters are preparing supper for our visitors at home so we must leave you now."

CHANGED PLACE NAMES

1787	1976
Wyoming	Wilkes Barre, Pa.
Fishing Creek	Bloomsburg, Pa.
Shamokin	Sunbury, Pa.
Delaware villages on the Allegheny	West Hickory, Pa.
Fort Pitt	Pittsburgh, Pa.
Lower Landing	Lewiston, N.Y.
Mouth of Credit	Port Credit, Ont.
Toronto River	Humber River, Ont.
Cataraqui	Kingston, Ont.
Oswegatchie and Point au Baril	Maitland, Ont.
Isle Royale	Chimney Is. N.Y.
Rapids Plat	
Aults Creek	Under waters of
Farran's Point	Lake St. Lawrence
Hoople Creek	on the Seaway
Long Sault Rapids	
New Johnstown	Cornwall, Ont.

MAIN SOURCE BOOKS

Pennsylvania

Balis, Samuel P.: Columbia and Montour County History; ed. by Battle

Stevens, S.K.: Outline of Pennsylvania History

Delaware Indians

Heckenwelder, John: Indian Nations

Tantaquidgeon, Gladys: Delaware Indian Medicine and Folk Beliefs

Zeisberger, David: History of N. A. Indians (Delaware)

Detroit

Burton, C.M.: History of Detroit

Catlin, George B.: The Story of Detroit

Palmer: Aspects of the Social History of Detroit

Hughes, Thomas: Journal for his Amusement

Quaife, Miles M. (ed): John Askin Papers

Voyageurs

Campbell, Marjorie Wilkins: The North West Company

Gibbon, John Murray: Romance of the Canadian Canoe

Great Lakes

Campbell, Marjorie Freeman: Niagara, Hinge of the Golden Arc

Robinson, Percy J.: Toronto Under the French Regime

Stanley: Historic Kingston and its Defences (Ont. Hist. Soc.)

Preston: Kingston Before the War of 1812

St. Lawrence

Croil, James: Dundas
Gray, Lillian Collier: Maitland, Seaway Village
Pringle, J. F.: Lunenberg or the Old Eastern District

Wild Food Supplies

Gibbons E. and McKay, David: Stalking the Wild Asparagus

Whitmore Massacre

Kirby, William: Annals of Niagara:
    Memoir of the Whitmore Family (Niagara Hist. Soc.)
Harris, George H.: Life of Horatio Jones
Balis, Samuel P.: Columbia and Montour County History
Gunn, Sarah W.: Captivity of Sarah Whitmore (Buffalo Hist. Soc.)
Portrait and Biographical Album, Iona and Montcalm Counties, Mich.
Freeze: History of Columbia County, Pennsylvania
Various unpublished papers in the Kirby, Whitmore and Hoople families.

Elizabeth Hoople is a great great granddaughter of Mary Whitmore Hoople. She was educated at Bishop Strachan School and the University of Toronto. She taught high school for some years, then later switched to writing and became the editor of the national magazine of the Canadian Girl Guides.

She makes her home in Streetsville, Ontario, where she lives with her poodle "Angus". In 1969 the Lions Club named her Citizen of the Year for her work with New Canadians. Her hobbies are sketching, gardening and genealogical research.

Besides the present work, Miss Hoople has published several short stories and a family history, *The Hooples of Hoople Creek.*

A MAP OF
MARY WHITMORE'S TRAVELS ××××

SCALE IN MILES
0 _____ 50